Stimulating Devotions for Church Groups

Amy Bolding

BAKER BOOK HOUSE

Grand Rapids, Michigan 49506

ISBN: 0-8010-0921-9

Fourth printing, April 1992

These devotions were selected from
Day by Day with Amy Bolding

Printed in the United States of America

Subject Guide

Abundant life 51

Bible 5, 56, 57, 89
Blessings 14, 102, 103, 106
Burdens, bearing each other's 57
Busyness 53

Childrearing 83
Christian living 21, 23, 58, 62, 68, 69, 72, 77, 82, 97, 100, 108, 121
Christmas 80
Church 68, 89, 95
Citizenship 15

Encouragement 116
Envy 91
Eternity, preparing for 33, 92, 122
Evangelism 6, 10, 20, 24, 26, 39, 43, 47, 62, 75, 77, 119

Faith 36, 98
Fellowship 31, 74
Forgiveness 31, 66
Freedom 7, 11

Giving 5, 23

God's direction 37, 46, 59, 71
God's love 40, 115
God's presence 25, 27, 52, 54, 76, 87, 100, 112, 113, 117
God's promises 41, 84, 86
God's provision 22, 49, 60, 66, 81, 93
God's purpose 32, 33
God's sovereignty 105
God's will 38, 39, 95
Gossiping 19, 44, 73

Helping others 8, 12, 16, 17, 28, 35, 79, 110
Heritage 10, 88
Holy Spirit 27
Hope 12

Jesus lives 41
Jesus' return 85
Judging others 78

Kindness 53, 63, 64, 97

Listening to Jesus 86
Lord's Prayer 92
Love 61, 107
Lying 67

Meditation 13
Memories 114

Obeying God 18, 90

Parents 45
Peace 99
Prayer 71, 73, 87, 118
Pride 70

Rest 113

Seeking God first 9, 15, 29, 59
Serving God 20, 30, 42, 49, 65,
   82, 94, 104, 120

Sin 8, 18, 51, 55, 64
Spiritual blindness 34
Success 55
Sunday observance 24
Surrendering to God 36

Thanksgiving 101, 105, 110, 111
Trials 48

Understanding others 79

Walking with God 75, 109
Work 47, 50, 107, 122
Worship 43, 96

The Art of Giving

The gifts of this world are trivial, but the gifts of Christ are beyond price. We can live without most of the superfluous things we get at Christmas but Christ is indispensable. Often people give to us because we gave to them. Christ gives to us because he loves us.

> Who profits most? 'Tis not the man
> Who, grasping every coin he can,
> Unscrupulously crushes down
> His weaker neighbor with a frown.
> He is not worthy of his trust,
>
> And friendless, knows his gold is dust.
> He loses what he sought to gain,
> And finds instead of pleasure, pain.
>
> Who profits most? It is not he
> Of life's great opportunity.
> He is not mourned — why should he be?
> Who shirks responsibility;
> Who, hermit like, himself withdraws
> To live apart from human flaws;
> To scoff at mortal frailties?
> He turns away — no vision sees.
>
> Who profits most? It is the man
> Who gives a boost where'er he can;
> Who's on the square in all that's done,
> And trusts and helps the others on;
> Who puts his task above mere self,
> And values friends, and counts them wealth.
> Who profits most? Is that your quest?
> It is the man who serves the best.

Prayer: Oh, God, may we this Christmas learn the art of giving ourselves. We pray in the name of one who gave all for us. Amen.

Hidden in Our Hearts

"Thy word have I hid in my heart, that I might not sin against thee." — Psalm 119:11

A wise sage has said: "If we would have the Bible in the heart we must first put it in the head."

Not long ago a four-year-old girl came to visit me. She asked me to be quiet so she could say the "Lord's Prayer." She had a queer way of pronouncing some of the longer words but she could repeat all the verses. Her baby sitter had taught her the words each afternoon when she put her to bed for her nap.

Another home I know well practices repeating verses of Scripture before the evening meal. The children are proud of the passages they have learned in this way.

In a Sunday School class we sing the following verse.

> I am so glad that our Father in heaven
> Tells of His love in the Book He has giv'n,
> Wonderful things in the Bible I see;
> This is the dearest, that Jesus loves me.
>
> I am so glad that Jesus loves me,
> Jesus loves me, Jesus loves me;
> I am so glad that Jesus loves me,
> Jesus loves even me.

Prayer: Help us this day, O God, to determine to hide thy words in our hearts — to make plans to share thy word with others — to live by the teachings found in thy Holy Book. We thank thee for the comfort and peace we find in reading the Bible. We pray in Jesus' name. Amen.

Whatever the Cost

"Preaching the kingdom of God, and teaching those things which concern the Lord Jesus Christ, with all confidence, no man forbidding him." — Acts 28:31

Paul had so much concern for the spread of the gospel that he suffered many things in order to spread the word. My favorite missionary is Adoniram Judson, an early-day missionary in Burma. Hardships seemed to be the only lot of the poor man, yet he would not give up. He was possessed with a burning desire to translate some of the New Testament into the language of the Burmese — a desire which almost caused him to lose his life. He had to spend many days in prison. In spite of all Adoniram's hardships, other young men in America, seeing his example, went to become missionaries also. They did not look at the hardships but rather kept their eyes on the goal to be reached.

> All ye saints of light proclaim,
> Jesus the light of the world;

Life and mercy in His name,
  Jesus the light of the world.
Hear the Saviour's earnest call,
  Jesus the light of the world.
Send the gospel truth to all,
  Jesus the light of the world.

We'll walk in the light, beautiful light,
  Come where the dew drops of mercy are bright;
Shine all around us by day and by night,
  Jesus the light of the world.

Prayer: Father in Heaven, help us to double our efforts to win unresponsive people to thy kingdom cause. Challenge us to spend our time showing a divine concern for the lost. In the name of Christ we pray. Amen.

Only God Can Keep Us Free

"Sing unto God, sing praises to his name: extol him that rideth upon the heavens by his name JAH, and rejoice before him." —Psalm 68:4

Over a century and a half ago some men met in Philadelphia. They declared the independence of our nation. The day was tense. Some of the brave statesmen made a few jests to try to ease the tension. Franklin said: "We must all hang together or we will all hang separately."

It is a time for great rejoicing and thanksgiving when a nation is free. But, there is no power to keep us free except the power of God. We may have the greatest number of weapons, and be the smartest people in the world, but we must have God on our side.

Did they finish the fight that day
  When the Liberty Bell was rung?
Did they silence the noise of war
  When Liberty's triumph was sung?
Was Freedom made sovereign indeed
  When the old bell pealed to the world
That the reign of oppression has ceased
  And the banner of freedom unfurled?
A battle has waged since the world was new;
  The battle is on, God calleth for you.

Prayer: O, Father, may we go forth to the fight in majesty today. Give us high-hearted fortitude and patience. Make us heralds of God's love. May we as Americans strive to be worthy of the fair name of our country. We pray in the name of the Prince of Peace, Jesus Christ. Amen.

The Dusty Path

"But let him that glorieth glory in this, that he understandeth and knoweth me, that I am the Lord which exercise lovingkindness, judgment, and righteousness, in the earth: for in these things I delight, saith the Lord." — Jeremiah 9:24

We had been traveling since early morning. Then we came to the Sunset Crater in Arizona. The road leading to the parking area is very restful and relaxing. When we were parked it seemed so good to get out and walk. We noticed a path leading up the side of the crater. Being in need of exercise we started walking, and the higher we went the more exciting the view became. We turned back before we reached the top. When we were back at the car we took stock. Our feet and legs were black from the dust of the burned lava which made up the path we had climbed. In our excitement we had not noticed what was happening to us.

Often in the excitement of some worldly pleasure we fail to notice its effect upon us until we are hopelessly soiled and defiled.

> O work thy works in God.
> He can rejoice in naught
> Save only in himself
> And what himself hath wrought.

Prayer: Dear Lord, our Master, we love thee and long to serve thee in the very best way. Draw us unto thyself. Take away from our lives the filth and grime of the sins of this world. Just for Jesus' sake we pray. Amen.

Be Ready for Service

"Come unto me, all ye that labor and are heavy laden, and I will give you rest." — Matthew 11:28

"But no one has asked me," we hear sometimes. Do we always have to be asked? Can't we volunteer? So many church members grow dull and cross complaining that they are not asked to do things. They should find a need and volunteer.

Sally was very angry with her best friend. She felt left out of a project on which her class was working. Sally felt her friend should have insisted that she help.

Mother was ashamed of Sally. That night she put a large platter of fried chicken right in front of Sally's plate. As soon as the blessing had been asked, Sally took her favorite piece off the top of the platter.

"Why Sally, you didn't wait for me to beg you to take some chicken," said Mother.

"Mommie, you know I don't have to be asked to take fried chicken," Sally laughed.

"You shouldn't have to be asked to help your class either," said Mother.

Sally got the point. Did you?

Prayer: Our Father, help us as thy children to volunteer to serve in places of need. May we not neglect the gift that is within us. This life is ours; help us to use it aright. We ask this in the name of the giver of life, Christ our Lord. Amen.

Keep to the Right

"Finally, brethren, whatsoever things are true, whatsoever things are honest, whatsoever things are just, whatsoever things are pure, whatsoever things are of good report; if there be any virtue, and if there be any praise, think on these things."

— Philippians 4:8

We must control our time, our activities, our thoughts.

"Why do you always keep your little dog on a leash?" I asked a neighbor child.

"Oh, if I didn't he would run away."

God knows our human weakness. So he warns us to keep our thoughts on the best things. God knows we would stray away from him if he gave us perfect freedom.

> Keep to the right, within and without,
>   With stranger and pilgrim and friend;
> Keep to the right and you need have no doubt
>   That all will be well in the end.
>
> Keep to the right in whatever you do,
>   Nor claim but your own on the way;

Keep to the right, and hold on to the true,
From the morn to the close of life's day!

Prayer: Heavenly Father, grant us power to look upon the world and see anew the things that are holy. We have so little time to spend on earth, help us make secure foundations for the life to come. Grant us the ability to see the best in our fellow man and praise him for that best. May our thoughts ever be directed toward things which will make the world a better place. We pray in the name of one who was always pure and perfect, Jesus Christ. Amen.

Our Task Is to "Tell It Out"

"Ye are the salt of the earth: but if the salt have lost his savor, wherewith shall it be salted? it is thenceforth good for nothing, but to be cast out, and to be trodden under foot of men."

— Matthew 5:13

Jesus gave us a task to perform, the task of spreading the gospel. He described Christians as salt and as light to spread the gospel and make the earth a better place.

Tell it out among the nations that the Lord is King;
Tell it out! Tell it out!
Tell it out among the nations, bid them shout and sing;
Tell it out! Tell it out!
Tell it out with adoration that He shall increase,
That the mighty King of glory is the King of Peace;
Tell it out with jubilation, let the song ne'er cease;
Tell it out! Tell it out!

— Frances R. Havergal

Prayer: Help us Lord to bring the good news of salvation to those who do not know thee. Grant that we may truly be as lights in this sin-darkened world. In the name of Christ we pray. Amen.

Let Us Be Worthy of Our Inheritance

"Forasmuch as ye know that ye were not redeemed with corruptible things, as silver and gold, from your vain conversation received by tradition from your fathers; But with the precious blood of Christ, as of a lamb without blemish and without spot."

— I Peter 1:18, 19

In the Mountain Lake Sanctuary at Lake Wales, Florida, stands the beautiful Singing Tower. The tower was erected by Edward

Bok. Edward came to America as an immigrant boy from Holland. For some reason the family had lost all they possessed and were very poor. Edward determined to win back for them a place in life of which they could be proud. He worked very hard writing books, editing a paper, and making himself a useful citizen during World War I.

When people go to the lovely Bok tower to rest and meditate, they cannot help remembering the little boy who fought such a hard life of poverty and hardship, to become famous and useful.

As Americans we have many wonderful traditions handed down to us from our forefathers. We must never take them as a matter of course but ever strive to be worthy of our heritage.

Prayer: Our Father, as we think of the great men who have made our nation a wonderful place in which to live, make us grateful. Help us always to seek to uphold the traditions of fair play and honesty. Just for the sake of Jesus. Amen.

True Freedom

"If the Son therefore shall make you free, ye shall be free indeed." — John 8:36

As Americans we have a multitude of freedoms that many people in the world do not enjoy. We have freedom to think and say what we please. We have freedom to worship in the church of our choice. We have freedom to move about from place to place as we please. We have freedom to try new ventures — and if we fail, to get up and try again. We were given these freedoms by those who went before us.

There is no freedom quite so wonderful as the freedom we received from Christ our Saviour — freedom from the yoke of sin.

> Looking upward every day,
>   Sunshine on our faces,
> Pressing onward every day
>   Toward the heavenly places.
> Growing every day in awe,
>   For thy name is holy;
> Learning every day to love
>   With a love more lowly.

Prayer: Dear Lord, as we think so often this month of the great freedoms we enjoy, make us truly grateful for the freedom given us by the Holy Son. Help us to hold up before our family high ideals. May we fight against the evil one who would conquer our hearts. May we ever draw nearer to thee. Have compassion, O God, on our human frailties. We ask in thy holy name. Amen.

Discouraged?

"For what shall it profit a man, if he shall gain the whole world, and lose his own soul?" — Mark 8:36

Often I remember a time when I was twenty-four. My husband was pastor of a very small church and he often makes more in a day now than he made in two weeks then. We were so poor that I think even the poor folks could call us poor. When I was the most discouraged I secured *The Life of Helen Keller* from the school library.

I think the babies were neglected a little while I devoured that book. When I had finished I faced the world with new courage. If one so handicapped could inspire and help others, why shouldn't I?

> They took away what should have been my eyes,
> (But I remembered Milton's Paradise)
> They took away what should have been my ears,
> (Beethoven came and wiped away my tears)
> They took away what should have been my tongue,
> (But I had talked with God when I was young).
> He would not let them take away my soul,
> Possessing that, I still possess the whole.

> — Helen Keller

Prayer: Dear Father, ruler of our destinies, give us always hope and courage. Help us always to remember our Bible, the symbol of hope, the direct word from thee. May we ever be mindful that the hope offered in the Holy Word transcends all human affliction with an overwhelming glory. We pray in the name of one who was all-glorious. Amen.

Always Something New

"These things I have spoken unto you, that in me ye might have peace. In the world ye shall have tribulation: but be of good cheer; I have overcome the world." — John 16:33

Many years ago in England, Dr. Thomas Withering watched an old gypsy woman gather some leaves from the garden and make a brew. She gave the mixture to people with swollen ankles and legs. From watching and experimenting, the medicine called digitalis was discovered. Many people with heart trouble have benefited from it.

A number of our most useful medicines and vaccines have been found by happy accidents. Penicillin was one of the greatest of these happy accidents.

We should never be too young or too old to keep alert for new discoveries and new thoughts.

> In every seed to see the flower,
> In every drop of dew
> To reverence a cloistered star
> Within the distant blue;
> To wait the promise of the bow,
> Despite the cloud between,
> Is Faith — the fervid evidence
> Of loveliness unseen.
>
> — John Banister Tabb

Prayer: Dear Father, as we bring ourselves before thee today, may we ever be ready to grow and develop into better people. May we seek the good of others and set forward thy kingdom. Inspire us with grace and truth. Help us to take advantage of every opportunity to show the fruits of the Spirit. For the sake of Jesus we ask. Amen.

The Blessings of Meditation

"Come ye children, hearken unto me: I will teach you the fear of the Lord. What man is he that desireth life, and loveth many days, that he may see good? Keep thy tongue from evil, and thy lips from speaking guile. Depart from evil, and do good; seek peace and pursue it." — Psalm 34:11-14

The beautiful Callaway Gardens at Pine Mountain, Georgia, is a nice place to go for quiet and meditation. At first people just walked about and enjoyed the lovely flowers and shrubs. Now there is a beautiful little chapel where one can go for a quiet moment of prayer and thought.

How very many hasty words and deeds would be left unsaid and undone if people took time for meditation before speaking or acting! Find a time and place for your own private talk with God each day.

In this hour of worship
   Grant thy presence, Lord!
Here, the world forgotten,
   Feed us on thy word.
From our sins and sorrows
   Here we seek release;
Of thy love persuaded
   Find the path of peace.

Prayer: Let the meditations of our hearts and the words of our mouths be acceptable in thy sight, O Lord, we pray. With reverent hopeful hearts help us to seek to know more of thy will in our lives. We ask these favors in the name of Christ our Redeemer. Amen.

Praise God for Our Blessings

"Bless the Lord God of Israel from everlasting to everlasting; and let all the people say, Amen, Praise ye the Lord."
— Psalm 106:48

It was Tom's first week at college and he was anxious to make friends. As he met new boys and girls he tried to remember the advice of his parents: "If you meet young people who are proud of their home town, church and family, they are usually worthy of friendship."

Tom was shocked at how many of his new acquaintances made fun of their home towns and wanted to be big shots.

One day as Tom walked across the campus he was homesick. Another boy fell in step beside him, "I wish you could see the trees in my home town this time of year."

"Are they large?" Tom asked.

"No," replied the boy. "The trees in our town do not grow too large because of the scarcity of rainfall. But I like them and miss them."

The two boys were soon fast friends and each told the other good points about their homes.

Since we deserve the name of friends,
   And thine effect so lives in me,
   A part of mine may live in thee
And move thee on to nobler ends.

— Tennyson

Prayer: Teach us, dear Father, the responsibility of being good citizens of our communities. Cause us to remember that others worked and toiled that we might have the blessings we now enjoy. Make us grateful. In the name of one whose presence will bless, Jesus Christ. Amen.

Focus on a Few

"Thou, which hast showed me great and sore troubles, shalt quicken me again, and shalt bring me up again from the depths of the earth." — Psalm 71:20

There are so many wonderful things in life that we must focus on a few and make the most of them. To make sure that we focus on the right things for our lives we must first seek the leadership of the Lord. Then we must read and study about the opportunities that the world affords. Twenty-five years ago we would have laughed anyone out of the room if they had said they wanted to fly around in space. We now have many more ways of finding the things on which people can focus their lives.

We should never think we are too smart to use the example of other people's past experience.

> I would be true, for there are those who trust me;
> I would be pure, for there are those who care;
> I would be strong, for there is much to suffer;
> I would be brave for there is much to dare.
>
> I would be friends of all — the foe, the friendless;
> I would be giving and forget the gift;
> I would be humble, for I know my weakness;
> I would look up — and laugh — and love — and lift.

Prayer: Our Father, help us to have a spirit of trust and love as we choose a focus for our lives. Help us to be teachable. We thank you for parents, teachers, friends and pastors who through our life have helped us to know right from wrong. We ask in Christ's name. Amen.

Citizens of Two Worlds

"And he said unto them, Whose is this image and superscription? They say unto him, Caesar's. Then saith he unto them, Render therefore unto Caesar the things which are Caesar's and unto God the things that are God's." — Matthew 22:20, 21

As Christians we are citizens of two worlds. We are indeed citizens of the present world. We usually live in a specific town, county, state, and nation. We owe to the government our loyalty and taxes.

But we are also citizens of the Kingdom of God. We are God's representatives here on earth. Often we have to stand against the crowd to uphold our beliefs for both our nation and our Heavenly Kingdom. As we spread the Kingdom of God we also help make our earthly world a better place in which to live.

> God only is the creature's home,
>> Though rough and straight the road:
> Yet nothing less can satisfy
>> The love that longs for God.
> How little of that road, my soul,
>> How little hast thou gone!
> Take heart, and let the thought of God
>> Allure thee further on.
>
> — F. W. Faber

Prayer: Father of all nations, help us to be good citizens of both our worlds. We would work to make our nation strong. Help us always to seek to bring in thy Kingdom. May we realize we are an example to others and be just the kind of example you would have us to be. We ask in the name of Jesus Christ. Amen.

The Hands of Christ

"He saved others; himself he cannot save. If he be the King of Israel, let him now come down from the cross, and we will believe him." — Matthew 27:42

"And when he had thus spoken, he showed them his hands and his feet." — Luke 24:40

Sitting next to a friend in church I noticed that even through her gloves large mishapen knots showed on her hands. The ugly mishaped hands did not look bad to me because I knew my friend was the cook for a large hospital. She cooked and also supervised the kitchen by day; at night she cared for an invalid mother. Her hands were hands dedicated to love.

Christ could have remained in heaven, but he chose to come to earth. He accepted the horror and shame of the cross for others — for us who are so unworthy.

> Have you failed in your plan of your storm-tossed life?
> Place your hand in the nail-scarred hand;

16

Are you weary and worn from its toil and strife?
Place your hand in the nail-scarred hand.

Are you walking alone through the shadows dim?
Place your hand in the nail-scarred hand;
Christ will comfort your heart, put your trust in Him,
Place your hand in the nail-scarred hand.

Is your soul burdened down with its load of sin?
Place your hand in the nail-scarred hand;
Throw your heart open wide, let the Savior in,
Place your hand in the nail-scarred hand.

Prayer: Dear Lord, help us ever to be aware that if we want to be happy we must place our hands in the hands of Christ. Make us willing to use our own hands to help others. We pray in the name of Jesus our Lord. Amen.

"Fret Not to Lose the Praise"

"The fear of the Lord is clean, enduring forever: the judgments of the Lord are true, and righteous altogether. More to be desired are they than gold, yea, than much fine gold: sweeter also than honey and the honeycomb." — Psalm 19:9, 10

Alfred was a big, strong boy and people often imposed on him. All year he had arrived at school early and helped the teacher get ready for the day. At the close of the school year the teacher gave out some small prizes to different pupils. She forgot to give one to Alfred. He felt discouraged, and decided he would just sleep later next year and not help.

When all the pupils assembled for the final chapel, the principal presented some awards. He called Alfred's name.

"For being the most co-operative and helpful boy."

Alfred was glad that even if the teacher hadn't noticed his helpfulness, the principal had.

> If thou hast thrown a glorious thought
>   Upon life's common ways,
> Should other men the gain have caught,
>   Fret not to lose the praise.
>
> Accept the lesson — look not for
>   Reward. From out thee chase
> All selfish ends — and ask no more
>   Than to fulfil thy place.

Prayer: Our Father, may we be ever mindful that we work on earth for the good of mankind. If we feel left out and forgotten, help us always to remember that thou art the one who judges our actions, our deeds and our works. Help us to be unselfish. We ask for the sake of Christ. Amen.

Obedience

"Do all things without murmurings and disputings: That ye may be blameless and harmless, the sons of God, without rebuke, in the midst of a crooked and perverse nation, among whom ye shine as lights in the world." — Philippians 2:14, 15

How we love to see a child who will go and perform his assigned tasks without murmuring or disputing. We say to ourselves, "What a nice child that is!"

Our Heavenly Father likes to see his children obey without complaint also.

> Some murmur when their sky is clear
>   And wholly brought to view,
> If one small speck of dark appear
>   In their great heaven of blue;
> And some with thankful love are filled
>   If but one streak of light,
> One ray of God's good mercy, gild
>   The darkness of their night.
>
> In palaces are hearts that ask,
>   In discontent and pride,
> Why life is such a dreary task,
>   And all good things denied.
> And hearts in poorest huts admire
>   How love has in their aid
> (Love that never seems to tire)
>   Such rich provision made.

Prayer: Our Father, who art so good to us, who each day gives us life and love and happiness, help us to banish discontent from our lives. May we ever sing a song of praise to thee. May we shine as the light of the world when we seek to tell others of thy great love. We ask in the name of Christ. Amen.

Sin's Allure

"Favor is deceitful, and beauty is vain: but a woman that feareth the Lord, she shall be praised." — Proverbs 31:30

When I was a little girl I liked to go to my grandmother's farm. My favorite pastime there was taking a pan of corn and coaxing the chickens to follow me. I would throw out just enough corn to make them follow me to a pen. Then I would put some corn in the pen and shut the door as quickly as I could. The chicken who was caught in the pen sometimes ended up in the frying pan. Sometimes I would enjoy the chicken as a pet for a while.

Sin allures us in just such deceitful ways. We are sure we are to get a nice reward, and suddenly we are caught in a net that does us harm — and sometimes destroys us.

> Lead us, O Father, in the paths of right;
> Blindly we stumble when we walk alone,
> Involved in shadows of a darksome night,
> Only with Thee we journey safely on.
>
> Lead us, O Father, to Thy heavenly rest,
> However rough and steep the path may be,
> Through joy or sorrow, as Thou deemest best,
> Until our lives are perfected in Thee.
>
> — W. H. Burleigh

Prayer: Our Father, the origin of all truth and reason, make our lives with thee like songs sung in gladness and joy. Use us as instruments to allure people to follow thee. We ask in the name of Jesus Christ our Lord. Amen.

Avoid Talebearers

"He that goeth about as a talebearer revealeth secrets: therefore meddle not with him that flattereth with his lips."

— Proverbs 20:19

Susie was talking to her close friend. The friend, burdened with worry, revealed to her that she was about to secure a certain position. In a few hours Susie was with another companion and revealed her friend's hope of securing the position. But she had revealed the fact to a false friend! In a few hours word had gone all around the little town. The man who had been about to hire Susie's friend decided something must be wrong, or so many people would not be talking about it.

Susie lost a friend, for never again would her friend speak to her. The friend lost the position and had to move to another city to find work. All this happened because someone was a tale-bearer.

He that shall rail against his absent friends,
Or hears them scandalized, and not defends,
Sports with their fame, and speaks what'er he can,
And only to be thought a witty man.
Tells tales, and brings his friends in disesteem,
That man's a knave, — be sure beware of him.

— Horace

Prayer: Father, make us aware of people with flattering lips. Help us to speak the truth and seek to build up all we know by kind words and loving deeds. We ask in the name of Christ. Amen.

Zeal for Winning the Lost

"Look down from heaven, and behold from the habitation of thy holiness and of thy glory: where is thy zeal and thy strength, the sounding of thy bowels and of thy mercies toward me? are they restrained?" — Isaiah 63:15

A minister who was growing old was admonished by his children to stop preaching so hard. His reply to them was, "I cannot rest while souls are lost in sin. I will have all eternity to rest in."

We should have zeal for our daily living. We should have zeal for winning the lost. We too can rest in eternity, and think of the reward for winning a soul to Christ.

Lead me to some soul today,
    Oh, teach me, Lord, just what to say;
Friends of mine are lost in sin,
    And cannot find their way.

Few there are who seem to care,
    And few there are who pray;
Melt my heart and fill my life,
    Give me one soul today.

— Will H. Houghton

Prayer: Almighty Father, keep us true to our best selves. Protect those we love today. Make us considerate of those about us and give us courage to witness to others of thy saving grace. We ask in the name of Jesus our Saviour. Amen.

Loyal for Service

"Let us not be weary in well doing: for in due season we shall reap, if we faint not." — Galatians 6:9

When her mother left to run some errands, Evelyn enthusiastically started to clean her room and get ready for company the next day. In about an hour she became tired and a little lonely. It would be nice just to telephone her friend Betty and chat for a few minutes.

When mother returned at noon Evelyn and Betty were still talking and laughing on the phone.

"But Evelyn, I depended on you to get the work done before our company came," exclaimed Mother.

Sometimes when we grow weary and think we are the only ones working for God we are tempted to stop and just waste a few days.

> I am only one,
> But still I am one.
> I cannot do everything,
> But still I can do something;
> And because I can not do everything,
> I will not refuse to do the something
> that I can do.
>
> — Edward Everett Hale

Prayer: O God, our Father, search our hearts today. Fill us with a desire to be sincere and truthful. May we worship thee with our whole heart. Give us a spirit of patience. May we ever be loyal in our service for thee. We ask in the name of our Saviour, Jesus Christ. Amen.

Working Together

"For as the body is one, and hath many members, and all the members of that one body, being many, are one body: so also is Christ." — I Corinthians 12:12

Leroy, an only child, was a member of the band. He played the clarinet very well. His mother thought him superior to all the other band members; so she was constantly going to the director and asking for Leroy to be given a solo part. The band director became very annoyed with the mother. He could not think of a way to show her that the band must work as a group, not as individuals.

Finally there came a day when the town was having a celebration and the band was going to march. The director talked with Leroy and they formed a plan.

As the fond mother stood on the curb watching for the band to come by she was amazed to see no sign of her darling child. Then after all the others had gone by, Leroy walked down the street all alone, blowing a sad little tune on his horn. The mother was so angry she rushed to the band director and was about to tear him apart.

"Isn't that what you wanted?" he asked her, "your child carrying on alone?"

Prayer: O Lord, may we be willing to be a part of thy kingdom. May we work with others to make the whole more perfect. We pray for Christ's sake. Amen.

God Makes Our Best Better

"I beseech you therefore, brethren, by the mercies of God, that ye present your bodies a living sacrifice, holy, acceptable unto God, which is your reasonable service." — Romans 12:1

It may not be our lot to wield
The sickle in the ripened field;
Nor ours to hear, on summer eves,
The reapers song among the sheaves;

Yet where our duty's task is wrought
In unison with God's great thought,
The near and future blend in one,
And whatsoe'er is willed is done!

And ours the grateful service whence
Comes, day by day, the recompense;
The hope, the trust, the purpose stayed,
The fountain and the noonday shade.

— Whittier

Isn't it wonderful that God asks that we present ourselves to him as we are? God does not say we must present our bodies *if* they are beautiful and agile, *if* our minds are well educated. If we give God the best we have he will, in time, make our best better. We will grow in grace and knowledge as our Lord wills us to do.

Prayer: Lord, may we today commit our lives to thee, and wilt thou make them count in thy service. May we find the best way to worship thee and the best way to serve. Give us fresh determination to be wholly thine. We ask in the name of Christ. Amen.

Rules of Behavior

"I will behave myself wisely in a perfect way. O when wilt thou come unto me? I will walk within my house with a perfect heart." — Psalm 101:2

When George Washington was a young boy he wrote some rules of behavior. In all his life, even after he had become president, he tried to follow these rules. Some of them are as follows:

"Every action in company ought to be with some sign of respect to those present."

"Sleep not when others speak; sit not when others stand; speak not when you should hold your peace; walk not when others stop."

"Be no flatterer; neither play with any one that delights not to be played with."

"Do not give your opinion unasked."

"Let your countenance be pleasant."

"Use no reproachful language against any one, neither curse, nor revile."

"Be not hasty to believe flying reports to the disparagement of any."

"Associate yourself with men of good quality."

Prayer: Dear Father, help us to grow in wisdom and dignity. May we make our character one of uprightness and model living. We ask in the name of the one perfect man, Jesus. Amen.

Giving What We Have

"Silver and gold have I none; but what I have that I give thee. In the name of Jesus Christ of Nazareth, walk. And he took him by the hand, and raised him up." — Acts 3:6, 7

Few of us have a great amount of money to give to those about us in need; but there are other gifts.

A young boy had run away from home because his father was a drunkard and often beat him. He came to a bridge and under it sought shelter from the cold. A small boy chasing his dog ran under the bridge and saw the older boy.

"Why are you here?" he asked.

"I have no place else to go and I am hungry and cold," the poor boy replied.

"Come to my house. My mother loves boys, and she will feed you."

So the two boys went to the humble farm home. True to her son's prediction the mother took in the runaway lad. She kept him for several years and he learned to work, and to love and be loved.

Prayer: Father, help us to look about and see those in need of love, of knowledge of thee, of comfort and strength. May we ever be willing to give of what we have to others. We ask in the name of Jesus. Amen.

Life's Prominent Business

"But be ye doers of the word, and not hearers only, deceiving your own selves." — James 1:22

As children of God one business should be predominant in our life. It is the soul-winning business. It is wonderful to go to church and hear a good message. It is still more important to go out and put that message into action. There is no Christian so weak or incapacitated that he cannot pray for the lost.

> Did Christ o'er sinners weep,
> And shall our tears be dry?
>
> Give me a faithful heart,
>   Likeness to thee,
> That each departing day
>   Henceforth may see
> Some work of love begun,
> Some wanderer sought and won,
> Some deed of kindness done,
>   Something for thee.

Prayer: Our Father, make us mindful of the lost world about us. May we always remember thy great commission and seek to carry out thy commandments. May our business in life be first of all to serve thee. We ask in the name of one who lived only to serve, Jesus Christ. Amen.

The Sabbath Day

"Remember the sabbath day, to keep it holy. . . . But the seventh day is the sabbath of the Lord thy God: in it thou shall not do any work, thou, nor thy son, nor thy daughter, thy manservant, nor thy maidservant, nor thy cattle, nor thy stranger that is within thy gates." — Exodus 20:8, 10

How rested and happy we feel when we spend Sunday in a quiet way — worshiping God and being grateful for home and family!

> Hail to the day which He, who made the heaven,
> Earth, and their armies, sanctified and blest,
> Perpetual memory of the Maker's rest!
> Hail to the day when He, by whom was given
> New life to man, the tomb asunder riven,
> Arose! That day His church doth still confess,
> At once Creation's and Redemption's feast,
> Sign of a world called forth, a world forgiven.
> Welcome that day, the day of holy peace,
> The Lord's own day! to man's creator owed,
> And man's Redeemer; for the soul's increase
> In sanctity, and sweet repose bestowed;
> Type of the rest when sin and care shall cease,
> The rest remaining for the loved of God!

Prayer: Father, help us to honor the Sabbath on earth. We want to share the joys of heaven when this life is o'er. May we be careful to obey thy commandments here and now. Give us the realization that in all thy commandments thou didst plan what was best for thy children. Give us ability and courage to stand for the right when so much of the world wants only the wrong. We ask in the name of Jesus Christ. Amen.

A Friend Forever

"For the Lord is good; his mercy is everlasting; and his truth endureth to all generations." — Psalm 100:5

One time we had some very dear friends. They would look after our place while we were on vacation and we would do anything we could for them. Suddenly they changed. They did not want to visit with us anymore and refused our friendship. We were deeply hurt because we did not know the reason why they treated us so strangely. We did not know why they ceased to be our friends.

God is a friend who never changes. Always he wants what is best for us; always he loves us and seeks to lead us aright.

> I have a friend indeed,
> A friend I often need,
> And when I need him he is always near,

To chide me when I'm wrong,
To fill my heart with song,
Or make the hidden way seem clear.

Now Jesus is his name,
His love is e'er the same;
And tho' my love for him may feeble grow,
Still thro' my tears I see
My friend awaiting me,
And hand in hand we onward go,

It is enough for me
To know that he will be
A friend when all the rest forget my name;
When thro' the gates of gold
My chariot wheels have roll'd,
He'll be my loving friend the same.

— C. Austin Miles

Prayer: Father make us mindful of the one true friend, we ask in his name. Amen.

Caring Enough

"The love of Christ constraineth us." — II Corinthians 5:14

One time in Virginia I heard a young lady play the piano in a concert. "How God has blessed her," I thought.

Later I made her acquaintance. To my amazement I found she practiced five hours each day. No wonder she could play; she cared enough about it to pay the price in practice.

A football player, injured in the game, begged the coach to let him go back and try again. Most great things in the world have been accomplished because someone cared enough to pay the price.

Our only purpose, as we live,
  Is something of ourselves to give
To others as they pass nearby —
  But what give I?

The painter paints for all to see,
  The singer gives a melody,
The rich upon cash gifts rely —
  But what give I?

I have no talents, large or small,
  Nor have I wealth; it seems that all

I have is love that cannot die —
And this give I.

— Dorothy Lee

Prayer: Our Father, help us to care about a lost world — a world in need of love. May we realize that poems die and music fades away but the soul lives on forever. May we care enough to win the lost. In his name we pray. Amen.

Ready Help Available

"But ye shall receive power, after that the Holy Ghost is come upon you: and ye shall be witnesses unto me both in Jerusalem, and in all Judaea, and in Samaria, and unto the uttermost part of the earth." — Acts 1:8

During the days when the dread disease polio stalked our land many people had to live in iron lungs. The iron lung was powered by electricity. In the hospitals there were battery powered units to be used in case the electricity went off for a few moments. In the homes where iron lung victims lived the family would have to work hand pumps to keep the patients breathing if the electric power failed.

As Christians we often feel that our power as God's children is very weak; but he has promised us "standby power" in the form of the Holy Spirit. We can call for help any time, day or night, and be assured that our prayer will be answered.

> God dropped a spark into everyone,
> And if we find and fan it to a blaze
> It'll spring up and glow like — like the sun,
> And light the wandering out of stony ways.

— John Mansfield

Prayer: Dear Father, giver of all power on earth and in heaven, help us always to call upon thy name in time of need. Give us the power we need to make our lives count in service for thee. We ask in the name of Jesus. Amen.

Something for Everyone

"Oh, that men would praise the Lord for his goodness, and for his wonderful works to the children of men!" — Psalm 107:8

To the artist He is the One Altogether Lovely.
To the architect He is the Chief Corner Stone.

To the baker He is the Living Bread.

To the banker He is the Hidden Treasure.

To the biologist He is the Life.

To the builder He is the Sure Foundation.

To the educator He is the Great Teacher.

To the farmer He is the Lord of the Harvest.

To the geologist He is the Rock of Ages.

To the jurist He is the Righteous Judge, the Judge of all men.

To the florist He is the Rose of Sharon and the Lily of the valley.

To the jeweler He is the Pearl of Great Price.

To the lawyer He is the Counselor, the Lawgiver, the Advocate.

To the horticulturist He is the True Vine.

To the newspaper man He is the Good Tidings of Great Joy.

To the oculist He is the Light of The World.

To the philanthropist He is the Unspeakable Gift.

To the philosopher He is the Wisdom of God.

To the preacher He is the Word of God.

To the sculptor He is the Living Stone.

To the servant He is the Good Master.

To the statesman He is the Desire of All Nations.

To the student He is the Incarnate Truth.

To the theologian He is the Author and Finisher of Our Faith.

To the traveler He is the New and Living Way.

To the toiler He is the Giver of Rest.

To the sinner He is the Lamb of God that taketh away the sin of the world.

To the Christian He is the Son of the Living God, the Saviour, the Redeemer and the Lord.

Prayer: Dear Father, help us to know in our own hearts what Christ means to us. Help us ever to trust in his salvation for our souls. We ask in his name. Amen.

The Blessing of Mercy

"For there is no distinction between Jew and Greek: for the same Lord is Lord of all, and is rich unto all that call upon him: for, Whosoever shall call upon the name of the Lord shall be saved." — Romans 10:12, 13

In a small town in a Western state there was discovered a man who had escaped from a prison in the East over twenty years before. He was arrested and carried back to the scene of his original crime. The people in the little western town were shocked; his wife and children were heartbroken. Then someone said: "Let's get up a petition. Let's show the governor back there what a good citizen our friend has been these twenty years." Name after name went on the petition. Then a friend made a trip to the East to take the petition to the governor personally, and to plead for mercy.

The governor was so touched by the loyalty of the man's friends that he did grant him a pardon and the man returned home.

> The wounds I might have healed,
> The human sorrow and smart!
> And yet it never was in my soul
> To play so ill a part.
> But evil is wrought by want of thought
> As well as want of heart.
>
> — Thomas Hood

Prayer: Father of all mercies, we ask thee to make us merciful to those in need. Make us kind to the friendless and ever grateful for the mercy thou hast showered upon us. For the sake of Christ we ask. Amen.

Heeding God's Call

"But seek ye first his kingdom, and his righteousness; and all these things shall be added unto you." — Matthew 6:33

> A hand in the dark clutched tight to my heart,
> A voice sounded close to my ear.
> A tear from his face dropped hot on my cheek;
> He breathed with the quickness of fear.
>
> The message he brought was a heart-rendering one
> Of darkness and pain, even death.
> And then with a hope he dared not express
> He waited with bated breath.
>
> "But why should I go? There are others to send
> And I have too much here to do."
> "O yes," he replied, "there are others I know,
> But they are exactly like you."

"But why should I go? You are nothing to me;
My friends and my family are here."
"O yes," he replied, "Then you'll understand
What it cost to lose those who are dear."

"But why should I go? I have God for myself;
I'll pray and I'll give when I please."
"O yes, that is true." And he sighed in despair,
"I had hoped to find one among these."
As he turned from my side he let my heart go
And it turned cold, even as stone.
My ears heard the silence, the tear burned my face
And I felt so terribly alone.

My call broke the silence. He quickly turned
To hear me say, "God I am Thine."
Together we went, and no loneliness felt
For His tears were mingled with mine.

Prayer: Our Father, make us mindful of thy call today. May
we be watchful for those in need of the gospel story. We ask
in the name of the living Christ. Amen.

Willing to Serve

*"The Son of Man came not to be served but to serve, and to
give his life a ransom for many."* — Matthew 20:28

Every day God is seeking laborers for his vineyard. He calls
young and old, and he offers all the same reward.

Churchill said to the British people during the World War II,
"I can promise you nothing but blood, sweat and tears."

It is only human to ask, "What will I have for this task?"

In Matthew 19:27, the disciples asked, "Lo, we have left everything and followed thee. What then shall we have?"

Many refuse the call to work in the Master's vineyard. Many
do not want to serve unless they are sure of a great reward. We
must examine our motives and be sure we have the right spirit
as we serve.

A few can touch the magic string,
And noisy Fame is proud to win them —
Alas for those who never sing,
But die with all their music in them.

Nay, grieve not for the dead alone
Whose song has told their heart's sad story —

Weep for the voiceless who have known
The cross without the crown of glory.

— Oliver Wendell Holmes

Prayer: God, give us the will to obey thy call. Help us to realize there is a task just for each of us. Make us willing to serve in the lowliest place as well as the highest. We ask in the name of him who served all. Amen.

The Fire of Fellowship

"Let us then pursue what makes for peace and for mutual upbuilding." — Romans 14:19

Tom was a teen-ager and he wanted very much to stay home on Sunday and read the paper, look at television and just loaf. "Why can't I worship here?" he asked.

It was Saturday night and the family had been enjoying a nice fire in the fireplace. Tom's father went to the fireplace and pushed the logs apart, and turned off the gas feeder.

"Why do that? We will be up another hour," Tom complained.

"Well, son, you see if the logs are separate and the power of the gas is turned off the fire soon dies out."

"I know, but why do it?"

"You are like the logs. If you go to services and stay close to the power of God and to the fellowship of other Christians, you keep burning bright for God."

Once to every man and nation comes the moment to decide,
In the strife of Truth with Falsehood, for the good or evil side;
Some great cause, God's new Messiah, offering each the bloom or blight,
Parts the goats upon the left hand, and the sheep upon the right,
And the choice goes on forever 'twixt that darkness and that light.

— James Russell Lowell

Prayer: Our Father, help us choose the right. Amen.

Ever Seek Forgiveness

"In him we have redemption through his blood, the forgiveness of our trespasses, according to the riches of his grace which he lavished upon us." — Ephesians 1:7, 8

31

Men may and do attend church in many different attitudes. Some have an attitude of reverence and worship. Others seem filled with an attitude of criticism; they see nothing beautiful or good about the services or the people present.

Some come seeking forgiveness for mistakes made. We should all do so. We should all lay aside the attitudes of arrogant self-sufficient pride and respond in reverence to Christ.

> God gives his child upon his slate a sum —
> To find eternity in hours and years;
> With both sides covered, back the child doth come,
> His dim eyes swollen with shed and unshed tears;
> God smiles, wipes clean the upper side and nether,
> And says, "Now, dear, we'll do the sum together!

Prayer: Dear Father, fill our souls with the forgiveness and love that overcomes all things bad and evil. In our own strength we can do nothing but we ask for thy strength and help today. In Christ's name we pray. Amen.

God's Plan for Us

"And the Lord make you to increase and abound in love one toward another, and toward all men, even as we do toward you."

— I Thessalonians 3:12

God has a plan for every life. God plans all things. He even has a perfect plan for the stars and planets. How do we find the perfect plan God has for us?

We need to read and study God's plan book, the Bible. We must make the right choices; the right companions will help us make these choices. We should never seek revenge when we feel we have been wronged. God will punish the wrong doer. We must learn to work as best we can and trust God for our provisions.

> Lord, help me have that perfect day,
>   That I may do your will, your way.
> Lord, help me do that perfect work,
>   And never the burdens of service shirk.
> Lord, help me have that perfect light.
>   And know your presence in darkest night.
> Lord, help me be a perfect friend
>   So that I might lift lives to begin again.
> Lord, help me have that perfect heart,
>   That Jesus' love it will impart.

> Lord, help me have that perfect love
> That my work here might count above.
> Lord, help me have that perfect day
> That I might walk the Jesus way.

Prayer: Father, help us to know that we will be judged by one who sees and knows all things. May we strive to have more love for our fellow man. Make us more obedient, willing servants. We ask in the name of Christ. Amen.

The Wrong Question

"In the day of prosperity be joyful, but in the day of adversity consider: God hath set the one over against the other to the end that man should find nothing after him." — Ecclesiastes 7:14

Sally awoke to see sunbeams shining across the floor of her room. But her face was not bright and sunny.

"What can I do in this dull place to have a good time?"

She started the day with the wrong question. Had she asked, "What useful work can I do today?" she would have been happier.

Each day God gives us something to do for his glory and the improvement of the world. It may be a small task; but if we are on the lookout for someone to help, someone to cheer — the hand of someone down and out, to grasp and lift up — then we will have joyful days and unknown strength.

> My heart leaps up when I behold
>   A rainbow in the sky:
> So was it when my life began;
> So is it now I am a man;
> So be it when I shall grow old,
>   Or let me die!
> The child is father of the man;
> And I could wish my days to be
> Bound each to each by natural piety.
>
> — William Wordsworth

Prayer: Father of all the earth, make our hearts to leap with joy as we behold the wonders of thy world. We ask in the name of one who was the wonder of wonders, Jesus. Amen.

Time Marches On

"When it is evening, ye say, It will be fair weather: for the sky is red. And in the morning, It will be foul weather to-

day: for the sky is red and lowering. O ye hypocrites, ye can discern the face of the sky; but can ye not discern the signs of the times?" — Matthew 16:2b, 3

Sometimes we grow so busy that we forget that time marches on and opportunities are lost. I heard the story of a small child who fretted because his father never attended Sunday School and church with him. His excuse was that he could not leave the small grocery store he owned.

"Mother, do you think daddy is a Christian?" asked the youngster.

"Yes, I hope so," the mother replied. "Why?"

"How will he get away from the store long enough to go to heaven?"

> All the long August afternoon,
>   The little drowsy stream
> Whispers a melancholy tune,
> As if it dreamed of June
>   And whispered in its dream.
>
> The silent orchard aisles are sweet
> Through the sere grass, in shy retreat,
> Flutter, at coming feet.
>   With smell of ripening fruit.
>   The robins strange and mute.
>
> There is no wind to stir the leaves,
>   The harsh leaves overhead;
> Only the querulous cricket grieves,
> And shrilling locust weaves
>   A song of summer dead.
>
> — William Dean Howells

Prayer: Father, we thank thee for the seasons of the year. We find something beautiful in each one. May we always find beauty in the seasons of our lives. In the name of Christ we pray. Amen.

Spiritual Blindness

"And they came to Jericho: and as he went out of Jericho with his disciples and a great number of people, blind Bartimaeus, the son of Timaeus, sat by the highway side begging." — Mark 10:46

Little Bobby took two nickles and held them over his eyes. "Look mommie, I can't see."

"Bobby I wouldn't do that. You should be so happy you are able to see," his mother replied.

Do we as Christians sometimes hold things of the world over our eyes and make ourselves blind to the joys and beauties around us? Do we let a little bit of jealousy keep us from enjoying the blessings of friendship with some people? We should seek to keep our spiritual eyes so bright we can enjoy all the wonders and beauties about us.

> Broken-hearted? No, you're not.
> You've too many blessings still
> That you know cannot be bought.
> See the good, forget the ill —
> Joy will come to you unsought,
> And abide with you until
> Earth becomes a beauty spot!

Prayer: Our Father, help us to realize there is a cure for spiritual blindness. There is the same cure the blind begger found beside the highway, the belief and love of Jesus Christ. May we like Bartimaeus call upon thee, Lord, for help and healing. We ask in the name of Christ. Amen.

Showing How Much We Care

"If any one has the world's goods and sees his brother in need, yet closes his heart against him, how does God's love abide in him?" — I John 3:17

How can we compare spiritual feeding and physical feeding? Yet both are mentioned in the Bible. We show how much we care for men's souls by the way we care for their bodies.

How can we show we care?

We can have compassion for the oppressed, visit the sick, show kindness to strangers. All the kind deeds in the world will not take the place of the blood of Jesus in the day of judgment if we have not believed on him.

> I dare not slight the stranger at my door,
> Threadbare of garb and sorrowful of lot,
> Lest it be Christ that stands; and goes His way
> Because I, all unworthy, knew Him not.

> I dare not miss one flash of kindling cheer
> From alien souls, in challenge glad and high.
> Ah, what if God be moving very near
> And I, so blind, so deaf, had passed Him by?

Prayer: Our Father, as we prepare for that great day of judgment when Jesus shall come in glory with a sceptre of righteousness, may it be with humble and grateful hearts. May we prepare for the receiving of heavenly rewards by serving thee on earth. We ask for the sake of Jesus our Saviour. Amen.

Operating on Faith Alone

"That the trial of your faith, being much more precious than gold that perisheth, though it be tried with fire, might be found unto praise and honor and glory at the appearing of Jesus Christ." — I Peter 1:7

George Muller was a famous English Christian. He felt led of the Lord to establish an Orphan-House. He had no money and planned to run the home on faith alone. In the year 1836 he started his venture. Many times God opened the way for food and clothing just at the right moment. I like to remember the time when Mr. Muller and the matrons had prayed until one o'clock in the night because there was not even a piece of bread for the children's breakfast. Finally, he started for home, tired and discouraged. For some reason he did not walk the path he usually took going home. As he walked along he met a man also walking.

Mr. Muller introduced himself and they walked along together. When they came to the place to part the new friend took out his purse and gave Mr. Muller ten pounds for the orphans. Can't you just see him getting up early the next morning to buy food for the orphans! But — can't you also see George Muller on his knees giving thanks to God!

Prayer: Dear Father, strengthen our faith. Help us to know thou art never asleep but always ready to answer our pleas. We ask in the name of Jesus Christ. Amen.

Almost All to Thee

"Humble yourselves therefore under the mighty hand of God, that he may exalt you in due time." — I Peter 5:6

As we read and study the Bible we sometimes want to surrender our lives to God — but not quite our whole lives. We want to retain our favorite sin, our favorite sport, or even just some time we can spend without any instructions from God.

If God has wrought a transforming experience of grace in our hearts, we will show evidence of surrender to him.

When we cease to struggle against God's will for us, then we know a real, glorious victory.

> All to Jesus I surrender,
> All to Him I freely give;
> I will ever love and trust Him,
> In His presence daily live.
>
> All to Jesus I surrender,
> Make me, Saviour, wholly thine;
> Let me feel the Holy Spirit —
> Truly know that Thou art mine.
>
> All to Jesus I surrender,
> Lord, I give myself to Thee;
> Fill me with Thy love and power,
> Let Thy blessing fall on me.
>
> — Judson W. Van De Venter

Prayer: Father in heaven, give us a changed heart that will be surrendered to thy will. Fill us with thy transforming power. May we ever respond to thy call and be truly surrendered Christians. We pray for Christ's sake. Amen.

Going Where God Leads

"By faith Abraham obeyed when he was called to go out to a place which he was to receive as an inheritance; and he went out not knowing where he was to go." — Hebrews 11:8

Every person wants to have a good name. Some want a great name enough to sacrifice and work for it. A name seldom comes by accident — usually by study, talent and work.

For Christian people their call usually comes from God. God has a purpose for our lives and he calls us for the fulfillment of that purpose. Like Abraham we must obey the call. We are not told how Abraham was called and we know all calls for service are not alike. Sometimes our service is just to witness to those about us in our home town. Sometimes it is to go far from home and serve in strange places.

One of the most attractive girls in our church felt called to go to Africa as a Journeyman Missionary. It almost broke her parents' hearts to see her go, but they prayed for God's will to be done. Her mother said, "We know she is safer in Africa if it is God's call than she would be in Texas against his will."

> It may not be on the mountain height,
>   Or over the stormy sea;
> It may not be at the battle front
>   My Lord will have need of me;
> But if by a still small voice He calls
>   To paths I do not know,
>
> I'll answer, "Dear Lord, with my hand in Thine,
>   I'll go where you want me to go."
>
> — Mary Brown

Prayer: Father, make us willing to follow thy call and go out not knowing where, but to serve. For Jesus' sake. Amen.

Father Knows Best

"He watereth the hills from his chambers: the earth is satisfied with the fruit of thy works." — Psalm 104:13

David and Danny had some small chickens and a mother hen. They were supposed to close the door to the pen securely each night to keep out harmful enemies of the chickens. Early each morning the chickens could be heard scratching and pecking at the door, wanting out. If the dew was heavy they were often kept in until the middle of the morning. If the day was nice they were out early to catch bugs and eat tender grass.

God knows when we need freedom, and when we need to be watched over closely. Often we peck away at some restraint and feel resentful; but God knows what is best for us.

> I know not where his islands lift
> Their fronded palms in air;
> I only know I cannot drift
> Beyond his loving care.
>
> — Whittier

Prayer: Father of all mankind, help us to know that thy dealings with thy children are always best. Oft we feel shut in and the way seems dark. Give us faith to know that when the time is right thou wilt open the door to better things. For the sake of Christ we pray. Amen.

Knowing Where the Deep Water Runs

"I know whom I have believed, and am persuaded that he is able to keep that which I have committed unto him against that day." — II Timothy 1:12

A passenger on a river boat was watching the pilot.

"How long have you been a pilot?" the passenger asked.

"I have been a pilot on these very waters for over thirty years," the man replied.

"Then by now you must know every rock and sand bar along the shores."

"Oh, no," the pilot replied. "I do not know anything like all the dangerous places along the shores."

"But how do you pilot the boat safely?"

"I know where the deep water runs and I pilot the boat in the deep water."

We may not know all the dangers along the shores of life, but we will be safe if we keep in the deep waters of God's will and love.

> Though I were hung on the highest hill,
> I know whose love would follow me still.
>
> Though I were drowned in the deepest sea,
> I know whose love would come down to me.
>
> — Old Ballad

Prayer: Lord our God, who searches our hearts for love and leads us in the way we should go, establish in us the desire to live ever close to thee. We ask in the name of Christ. Amen.

Harvest Time

"Say not ye, There are yet four months, and then cometh harvest? behold, I say unto you, Lift up your eyes, and look on the fields; for they are white already to harvest." — John 4:35

We planted just a few tomato vines, but they grew so profusely that our back yard was overrun with tomatoes. We were kept busy giving away tomatoes to our friends and neighbors. When they were ripe they had to be harvested quickly or they would be ruined. At times I suspected that there were field mice nibbling off the ripe ones.

Jesus was talking about a harvest of lost souls. They, too, are everywhere. They, too, must be harvested at the proper time or it may be too late. Even like the mouse nibbling at the tomatoes, Satan is ever ready to devour souls.

> Why do you wait, dear brother,
>   Oh, why do you tarry so long?
> Your Savior is waiting to give you
>   A place in His sanctified throng.
>
> What do you hope, dear brother,
>   To gain by a further delay?
> There's no one to save you but Jesus,
>   There's no other way but His way.
>
> — George F. Root

Prayer: Our Father, Lord of the harvest, help us today to look on the fields and go forth to reap. Show us the paths you would have us take to serve thee best. We pray in the name of Christ our Saviour. Amen.

God's Love

"For God so loved the world, that he gave his only begotten Son, that whosoever believeth in him should not perish, but have everlasting life." — John 3:16

We have all heard the story of the little girl who came home from Sunday School and told her mother, "We studied about God's only forgotten son today."

God still loves us and longs for us to come to his only begotten son. He could have asked us to perform all kinds of rituals in order to be saved, but he only asks us to believe. He could have said "only the people of one nation, or one race"; but he said, "Whosoever." This means that all who believe — regardless of nation, or race, or social status — will be saved.

And his gift of love is the same for all who believe, "everlasting life."

> Love sent my Savior to die in my stead,
> Why should he love me so?
> Meekly to Calvary's cross He was led,
> Why should He love me so?
>
> Nails pierced His hands and his feet for my sin,
> Why should He love me so?
> He suffered sore my salvation to win,
> Why should He love me so?
>
> Oh how He agonized there in my place,

Why should He love me so?
Nothing witholding my sin to efface,
Why should He love me so?

— Robert Harkness

Prayer: Father in Heaven, we are silent before thy great love. We are so unworthy of such sacrifice. Enable us to worship thee in spirit and in truth. We ask in the name of Christ. Amen.

God's Promises

"Whereby are given unto us exceeding great and precious promises." — II Peter 1:4

As believers we have a peculiar treasure in God's promises. We are very wealthy if we believe and carry out the conditions of God's promises.

There is a story told about when Abraham Lincoln was entertaining a friend in the White House. The friend coaxed one of the children to come and sit on his lap saying, "I will give you this watch fob if you will."

The child went to the man and sat quietly on his lap. When the friend was ready to leave President Lincoln reminded him he had not given the child the watch fob.

"Oh, I could not do that," replied the friend. "This is an old family heirloom."

"Then never come to my home again. I do not wish my children to know I entertain liars." The President sent the man away.

Yet in the maddening maze of things,
And tossed by storm and flood,
To one fixed trust my spirit clings:
I know that God is good!

— Whittier

Prayer: Our Father, we thank thee that thy promises are true. We thank thee most for the coming of the promised Saviour of the world. For it is in his name we pray. Amen.

Christ Lives and Reigns

"Worthy is the Lamb who was slain, to receive power and wealth and wisdom and might and honor and glory and blessing!"

— Revelation 5:12 (RSV)

When we read that the Lamb was slain, we know his mission on earth has been finished. Christ has been appointed the heir of all things. So we know he is reigning in heaven. Hebrews 1:3 reads: "He reflects the glory of God and bears the stamp of his nature, upholding the universe by his word of power. When he had made purification for sins, he sat down at the right hand of the Majesty on high."

I serve a risen Saviour, He's in the world today;
I know that He is living, whatever men may say;
I see His hand of mercy, I hear His voice of cheer,
And just the time I need Him He's always near.

Rejoice, rejoice, O Christian, lift up your voice and sing
Eternal hallelujahs to Jesus Christ the King!

The hope of all who seek Him, the help of all who find,
None other is so loving, so good and kind.

He lives, He lives, Christ Jesus lives today!
He walks with me and talks with me along life's narrow way.
He lives, He lives, salvation to impart!
You ask me how I know He lives:
He lives within my heart.

— Alfred Ackley

Prayer: Father in heaven, help us today to see all things through the eyes of faith and tell others of the reigning Christ. We pray in the name of Jesus. Amen.

"Go There and Take Him with You"

"Truly, truly, I say unto you, he who believes in me will also do the works that I do; and greater works than these will he do, because I go to the Father." — John 14:12

A young man who had recently surrendered to become a minister, went to his pastor and said: "How can I serve Jesus. I just must find a way to start my service."

"Look all around you and find some place where he is not. Go there and take him with you," the pastor replied.

Before we can work great works for Christ we must get our eyes off our selves. Then we must recognize that we have a responsibility and the world has a need.

No one else can witness for you,
    Nor can others flash your smile;
None can do what you're supposed to
    As you tread life's blessed mile.

For your deeds you have to answer
　　For each neglect you give account.
You're the one whom God has chosen
　　That assignment to fulfil.

With habits still unfrozen
　　Follow now his blessed will.

— J. T. Bolding

Prayer: Father, give us the courage to be free from doubt. Help us to seek thy will in our lives and go forward with a vision to accomplish thy purpose. We ask in the name of Jesus. Amen.

"Good-bye God"

"God is a spirit, and they who worship him must worship in spirit and in truth." — John 4:24

In Dallas, Texas, a few years ago a father, mother and four children attended Sunday School and church regularly. Then the father obtained a better job and they bought a new car. Each Sunday it seemed more convenient to get into the new car and go visit friends or relatives than to attend church.

One Sunday they passed the church as the people were gathering for services. The little five-year-old in the back seat leaned out the window and called, "Good-bye, God. We have a new car and don't need you any more."

The father and mother were convicted of their neglect and the following Sunday found them back in their old places in God's house.

Faithfully faithful to every trust,
　　Honestly honest in every deed,
Righteously righteous and justly just;
　　This is the whole of the good man's creed.

Prayer: Help us, our dear Lord, ever in word and deed to own thee as our Lord and Saviour. Amen.

Tomorrow I'll Tell the Story

"As it is written in the prophets, Behold, I send my messenger before thy face, which shall prepare thy way before thee."

— Mark 1:2

Around the corner I have a friend
In this great city that has no end,
And he is lost — a fine strong man,
But he is lost! And I always plan
To speak to him about God's love,
Of Christ who came down from above —
And of how he died on the cross to pay
The sinner's debt. I think each day
"Somehow I must speak my heart to Jim:
Tomorrow I'll have a talk with him."

Tomorrow comes, and crowding cares
Clutter my day with busy affairs.
The day is done and again I vow
Tomorrow I'll speak to Jim somehow.
For my friend is lost: he does not know
The peril he risks; he must not go
Year after year like this and die
Before I tell him how truly I
Desire to see him give his heart to Christ,
Repent, believe, and make a new start.
But tomorrow comes and tomorrow goes
And the distance between us grows and grows.
Around the corner! Yet miles away —
    "Here's a telegram, sir. . . .
    Jim died today."
While I delayed, thus came the end:
Jim lost a soul; Christ lost a friend!

                      — C. T. Towne

Prayer: O Thou who art the Saviour of all who trust in thee, forgive us for our neglect in telling the story of thy love. Make our witness acceptable unto thee. We ask in the name of our precious Saviour. Amen.

Guard Your Tongue

"I said, I will take heed to my ways, that I sin not with my tongue: I will keep my mouth with a bridle, while the wicked is before me." — Psalm 39:1

Two friends were whispering in church. They could not understand each other correctly. They should have been worshiping. One went away and told what she thought she had heard. The other friend heard what she told and became very angry. They had such an ugly quarrel that one changed her church membership to avoid seeing her one-time-friend again. All because they gossiped in church!

> Alas! they had been friends of youth:
> But whispering tongues can poison truth;
> And constancy lives in realms above;
> And life is thorny; and youth is vain;
> And to be wroth with one we love
> Doth work like madness in the brain.
> And thus it chanced as I divine,
> With Roland and Sir Leoline!
> Each spoke words of high disdain
> And insult to his heart's best brother;
> They parted — ne'er to meet again!
> But never either found another
> To free the hollow heart from paining.
> They stood aloof, the scars remaining.
> Like cliffs which had been rent asunder;
> A dreary sea now flows between,
> But neither heat, nor frost, nor thunder
> Shall wholly do away, I ween,
> The marks of that which once hath been.
>
> — S. T. Coleridge

Prayer: O almighty and everlasting God, be merciful to us. We are so hasty in our speech; we make so many mistakes. Turn us from our careless ways and strengthen us as Christians. Make us joyful in well doing. We pray in the name of Jesus Christ. Amen.

Worthy of Honor

"Honor your father and your mother." — Exodus 20:12

Home life in America today is too often like that described in the poem Longfellow wrote.

> Ships that pass in the night, and speak each other in passing,
> Only a signal shown and a distant voice in the darkness;
> So on the ocean of life we pass and speak one another,
> Only a look and a voice, then darkness again and a silence.

More and more parents spend less and less time with their children. We think of the commandment as being given to children, but parents also have an obligation. Parents must deserve honor.

45

We are given the promise of long days upon the earth if we honor our parents. When I was a very young girl I met a woman who seemed old to me then. She was always telling what wonderful people her parents had been and her grandparents before them. I often thought, "This woman will certainly live a long time; she honors her parents so much."

Sure enough, after I felt myself old, she was still living. She was very near ninety — and still bragging about her people.

Jesus set an example of honor by asking someone to care for his mother when he was dying.

Prayer: Father, as parents make us worthy of honor; as children make us glad to honor our parents. For Christ's sake. Amen.

Accepting the Future

"Jesus therefore, knowing all things that should come upon him, went forth, and said unto them, Whom seek ye?"
— John 18:4

When I was a girl just eighteen years old standing before the minister to be married, I did not know all the problems marriage carried with it — the mountains of dishes to be washed, all the floors to be swept, the babies to be cared for. Yet I doubt if I would have turned away had I known.

Christ knew he was soon to go to the cross, and he knew the suffering he would be forced to go through before he could cry, "It is finished." Yet knowing all this he went on, for our sake.

> Among the things that this day brings
>   Will come to you a call,
> The which, unless you're listening,
>   You may not hear at all.
> Lest it be very soft and low,
> What'er you do, where'er you go,
>   Be listening!
> Then whatsoe'er the call may be,
>   To service small or great,
> To cross the seas and speak God's love,
>   To smile, to rule a state —
> When God shall come and say to you,
> "Here is the thing that you must do,"
>   Be listening!

Prayer: Father, today let nothing keep us from listening for thy call. Knowing life will not always be easy; grant us the will to go on in service and love. We pray in the name of Jesus Christ. Amen.

"You Are the Hand"

"How sweet are thy words unto my taste! yea, sweeter than honey to my mouth!" — Psalm 119:103

Isn't it wonderful for a friend to say, "I have been thinking of you?"

A man lived next door to an unsaved man. Mr. King often prayed for his neighbor. One day he was earnestly praying, "God, lay a hand on my friend. Save his soul."

Suddenly a voice just seemed to say, "You are the hand. You are the hand; go and touch him."

Mr. King immediately went next door and began to pour out his heart — pleading with his friend to trust Christ.

After he was gloriously saved, the friend said, "I often wondered why you didn't ask me to go to your church."

'Tis the human touch in the world that counts,
    The touch of your hand and mine,
Which means far more to the fainting heart
    Than shelter and bread and wine;
For shelter is gone when the night is o'er,
    And bread lasts only a day,
But the touch of the hand and the sound of the voice
    Sing on in the soul alway.

— Spencer Free

Prayer: Our Father, help us ever to have the sweet taste of thy love in our hearts. Make us realize there are lonely people who need thy love. Make us the hands to lead them to thee. We pray through Jesus our Lord. Amen.

No Time for Idleness

"And about the eleventh hour he went out, and found others standing idle, and saith unto them, Why stand ye here all the day idle?" — Matthew 20:6

A lazy man was begging help for his family, saying he could not find food and clothing for his family.

"Nor can I," replied an industrious mechanic. "I have to work for it."

Too many people in our world today are standing idle. It seems easier to hold out a hand and be fed by others than to work for food and clothing.

Christians also sometimes grow lazy and merely want to sit in services and be fed, rather than getting out and working to bring new souls into the Kingdom of God.

> The heights of great men reached and kept
> Were not attained by sudden flight;
> But they, while their companions slept,
> Were toiling upward in the night;

So in the matter of working he will succeed best who takes most pains, who has no time for idleness.

Prayer: Our Father, give us the courage to work — for our families, for our church and most of all for thee. We ask in the name of thy dear Son. Amen.

Strength Replacing Weakness

"And he said unto me, My grace is sufficient for thee: for my strength is made perfect in weakness. Most gladly therefore will I rather glory in my infirmities, that the power of Christ may rest upon me." — II Corinthians 12:9

It is not the comforts of life that make us strong, but the trials. How we overcome the trials and handicaps tells the story of how we meet life.

It is said that the engineer who planned the great Brooklyn Bridge in New York, became a bedfast invalid before the bridge could be finished. He did not give up. He had a powerful telescope brought in and from his bed he kept close watch on the progress of the bridge. His body was weak but his mind remained sharp and active.

> It may be I shall never rise
> To place or fame beneath the skies —
> But walk in straitened ways till death,
> The narrow streets of Nazareth.
>
> But if through honor's arch I tread
> And there forget to bend my head,
> Ah! let me hear the voice which saith,
> "Mine were the streets of Nazareth."

When I am tempted to repine
That such a lowly lot is mine,
There comes to me a voice which saith,
"Mine were the streets of Nazareth."

Prayer: O thou who art the Saviour of those who trust in thee, make us strong in thy strength. Help us overcome weakness and fear. We ask in thy holy name. Amen.

Faithfully Serving Him

God fulfilled his promise by sending Christ from among the ranks of the children of Israel.

Two girls were promised a nice gift by their mother. There were some strings attached to the gift. They were to clean the house each Saturday until Christmas. Then they would receive the gift, some money for their own use in shopping.

Sometimes the girls wanted to run and play, or sit and look at television on Saturday but they would remember the promise of their mother and first clean the house.

O Word that broke the stillness first,
    Sound on! and never cease
Till all earth's darkness be made light,
And all her discord peace.
Till selfish passion, strife and wrong,
Thy summons shall have heard,
And thy creation be complete,
O thou Eternal Word.

— Longfellow

Prayer: Our Infinite Father, give us busy hands to help forward the time when all promises shall be fulfilled. Give us a spirit of love and gladness as we think of the prophecies given and fulfilled. Make us willing to serve thee more. We pray in Jesus' Name. Amen.

Light Behind the Dark Clouds

"And we know that all things work together for good to them that love God, to them who are the called according to his purpose." — Romans 8:28

William was determined to make a minister. He felt sincerely in his heart that God had called him. His parents were very poor and could not help him go to school. He borrowed a few dollars and with all he possessed tied in a pasteboard box he went to a college. It happened that the very day he arrived someone had resigned in the maintenance department. He was given the job. Often during the years that followed William was tired but always he pushed on because he felt God was with him.

> Never, not since the world began
> Has the sun ever once stopped shining.
> His face very often we could not see,
> And we grumbled at his inconstancy,
> But the clouds were all to blame, not he,
> For, behind them, he was shining.
>
> And so, behind life's darkest clouds
> There's something always shining.
> We veil it at times with faithless fears,
> And dim our sight with foolish tears,
> But in time the atmosphere always clears,
> For there's something always shining.

Prayer: Our Father, who hast declared thy love to all men, may we ever rest in the knowledge that all things do work together for good; that thou art ruling the world and art our friend. We ask in the name of Jesus. Amen.

Ordinary Tasks

"Man goeth forth unto his work and to his labor until the evening." — Psalm 104:23

"Thou hast blessed the work of his hands, and his substance is increased in the land." — Job 1:10b

A boy I knew some years ago went out to find a job. He had been a paperboy and had done his work well — and had enjoyed it. But now he wanted something more important. Soon he secured a job for after school and for the summer. He was very happy and came rushing home to tell his mother. After that he had increasingly larger and better jobs — but he appreciated each one. He always counted it a privilege to have a place to work.

The world is made up of people who do just common ordinary tasks and who are proud to be working.

> My Master was a worker
> With daily work to do,
> And he who would be like Him
> Must be a worker too;
> Then welcome honest labor

And honest labor's fare,
For where there is a worker
The Master's man is there.
—W. C. Tarrent

Prayer: Our Father, make us proud of being able to engage in honest labor. May we never sell principle for popularity in our work. We thank thee for the ability to toil, and ask thee to bless those who are ill or unable to find places to labor. We pray in the name of one who toiled each day to bring the Kingdom of Heaven to earth. Amen.

Aiming High

"Nay, in all these things we are more than conquerors through him that loved us." — Romans 8:37

Jill wanted to be popular on her college campus. She was a Freshman and as yet had not met many of the students. Then she heard there was to be a contest for a Freshman Queen. She decided that she would enter the contest.

"You are not from a rich family," her roommate objected. "You do not go out for some of the social affairs on campus. I would say you are too religious to win a contest."

"I intend to try for it," Jill replied. "People will know me as I am when the contest is over."

When Jill was through making her own posters and going all over campus with them, she had made many friends. They respected and liked her exactly as she was. When the final day arrived she was in the top ten and ended the contest by being next to the queen.

It is not always what we hit, but what we aim at, that helps us grow as people.

Jill thought she could be a queen and she became a princess.

Prayer: Father, we all have unfulfilled dreams and desires. Help us to know we can find completeness and happiness in thee. In our own strength we often are failures but with thy strength we can reach the unattainable. For Christ's sake we pray. Amen.

Running from Temptation

"Then saith Jesus unto him, Get thee hence, Satan: for it is written, Thou shalt worship the Lord thy God, and him only shalt thou serve." — Matthew 4:10

Jesus knew when he was being tempted. He knew when he was in the wrong company and asked that company to leave.

Often the best way to get away from temptation is to run from it.

A little girl was picking and eating ripe strawberries. Her mother had forbidden her to eat the strawberries because she was allergic to them. She thought no one would know. As she was about to leave the strawberry bed she tripped on a vine and fell. When she got up a large stain was on the front of her dress.

> What matter if I stand alone?
>   I wait with joy the coming years;
> My heart shall reap where it hath sown,
>   And garner up its fruits of tears.
> The waters know their own, and draw
>   The brook that springs in yonder heights;
> So flows the good with equal law
>   Unto the soul of pure delights.

Prayer: O God, forgive us when we are weak and descend to temptation. Help us to walk in the way of Jesus Christ, and follow his example of putting aside temptation. We ask in the name of Jesus. Amen.

Awareness of God's Works

"O Lord, how manifold are thy works! in wisdom hast thou made them all: the earth is full of thy riches." — Psalm 104:24

Teddy was watching an ant bed. Sometimes he would take a piece of straw and push an ant away from the opening to the ant hill.

"Mother, do I seem as small to God as the ants do to me?"

"I am sure you probably are much smaller," his mother told him. "But you are better off because God wants everything good for you and sometimes I see you kill the ants."

> Alas, my God, that we should be
>   Such strangers to each other!
> O that as friends we might agree,
>   And walk and talk together!
>
> May I taste that communion, Lord,
>   Thy people have with Thee?

Thy Spirit daily talks with them,
O let It talk with me!

Like Enoch, let me walk with God,
And thus walk out my day,
Attended with the heavenly Guards,
Upon the King's highway.

When wilt Thou come unto me, Lord?
For till Thou dost appear,
I count each moment for a day,
Each minute for a year.

— Shepherd

Prayer: O Lord, we humbly beseech thee, open our eyes to behold thee in all thy love and glory. Open our lips that we may magnify thy name. We pray in the name of Jesus. Amen.

Too Much Going On

"And as thy servant was busy here and there he was gone."
— I Kings 20:40

All American parents and children seem to be busy here and there. Do we ever stop to see what is going from our lives while we are so busy? A young mother told me her children had so many extra-curricular activities she was never home nights. She was always busy taking them places. She belonged to that growing group of families where the mother as well as the father has a car. Sometimes she said the children were so busy she took one in one direction and the father took another some place else. People that busy are losing all the sacred fellowship God meant for homes to have.

We school our manners, act our parts,
But He who sees us through and through
Knows that the bent of both our hearts
Was to be gentle, tranquil, true.

— Matthew Arnold

Prayer: Our Father, help us today to hunger and thirst after righteousness. May we seek to be more like the Master. Help us not to be so busy about worldly affairs that we lose sight of thee. We ask in Jesus' name. Amen.

Loving Words Cost Little

"The fear of the Lord is the beginning of wisdom: a good

understanding have all they that do his commandments: his praise endureth forever." — Psalm 111:10

One Sunday morning I had been given a message for our pastor's wife. Nothing else seemed to be on my mind except that I give her the message after services. Hurrying down to where she stood I passed two people I should have spoken to, but ignored completely. After I had delivered my message I thought how rude I had been. Hurrying back to find them I apologized but I could tell they were hurt. We certainly need to develop wisdom in the way we speak and act with our friends.

> Loving words will cost but little,
>   Journeying up the hill of life;
> But they make the weak and weary
>   Stronger, braver, for the strife.
> Do you count them only trifles?
>   What to earth are sun and rain?
> Never was a kind word wasted;
>   Never was one said in vain.

Prayer: Our Father, may the testimony of our lips and the testimony of our lives be acceptable in thy sight. Help us today to say something that will lead someone to a closer walk with thee. We ask in the name of Jesus Christ. Amen.

The Garden of Our Hearts

"The eyes of the Lord are in every place, beholding the evil and the good." — Proverbs 15:3

Pansy had big brown eyes and black hair. She had worked very hard making a little garden in a flower bed. She had some onions and some carrots almost ready to eat. She thought about how proud of her the family would be when she served them. Then one day when she came home from school a dog had dug up almost all her carrots and scattered them about.

Pansy's mother found her sitting on the back step weeping. After they talked about the dog and how he destroyed her garden mother brought up another subject.

"Pansy, did you know your heart is God's garden. He wants only good thoughts and deeds to grow there." She put her arm tight around Pansy, "Sometimes the devil comes and tries to destroy God's garden by pulling up the good thoughts and planting bad ones. We are the ones who must be very careful that no one destroys the good in the garden of our hearts."

The fear of God and sweet content
Yield riches that will ne'er be spent.

Prayer: Dear God, help us to keep our hearts pure and holy for thy service. Make us strong against the wiles of the devil. We ask for Christ's sake. Amen.

Paying the Price

"Blessed are ye, when men shall revile you, and persecute you, and shall say all manner of evil against you falsely, for my sake." — Matthew 5:11

Most people want to achieve success in life; only a few are willing to pay the price. There are always fences to climb over on the road to success. There are sacrifices of time and effort to be made. There are those who would hold others back because they are too lazy to seek success. A successful person is one who has overlooked the locked gates and the hands trying to hold him back. He has climbed over the fences with hard work and faith in his ability.

Take a dash of water cold
And a little leaven of prayer,
A little bit of sunshine gold
Dissolved in the morning air;
Add to your meal some merriment
And a thought for kith and kin;
And then, as a prime ingredient
A plenty of work thrown in:
But spice it all with the essence of love
And a little whiff of play:
Let a wise old book and a glance above
Complete a well spent day.

Prayer: Our Heavenly Father give us today the perseverance in prayer and work to make our lives successful for thee. In James we are promised, "the effectual fervent prayer of a righteous man availeth much." Make us worthy to claim that promise. We ask in Jesus' name. Amen.

The "Little" Sins

"Take us the foxes, the little foxes, that spoil the vines: for our vines have tender grapes." — Solomon's Song 2:15

We had a lovely tree growing on the back of our lot. I have often thought, "What a fine, strong tree."

Then one day my small son came hurrying in the house, "Mother, the tree on the back fence has fallen over."

Heartbroken we went out to see our lovely tree broken off almost even with the ground. Some kind of a bug or worm had eaten the heart out and just a little gust of wind had blown it over.

So often lives are harmed and ruined, not by big sins but by little ones that eat and gnaw until all the heart is infested and ruined. Just a small wind of adversity can then destroy us.

> And when he fell in whirlwind, he went down
> As when a lordly cedar, green with boughs,
> Goes down with a great shout upon the hills,
> And leaves a lonesome place against the sky.
>
> — Edwin Markham

Prayer: Father, may we today realize life is not made up of great deeds of valor, but of little duties faithfully carried out day by day. May we make the world a better place by showing little kindnesses to those about us, giving smiles and comfort to those who are lonely. We pray in the name of Jesus. Amen.

The Unchangeable Book

"Open thou mine eyes that I may behold wondrous things out of thy law." — Psalm 119:18

When Gordon's father was reading the Bible at the breakfast table he talked about all the wonderful things in the world today. He could hear the washing machine running in the utility room and so he mentioned how nice that Mother did not have to draw water and heat it in a pot and rub clothes on a rub board.

"Daddy, is there anything that has not been invented new in this great age?" Gordon asked.

"Yes, there are many things man has not improved upon," Father told him. "We cannot change the moon, the stars, or the sun. We cannot find a book better able to guide us than the Bible."

> We search the world for truth, we cull
> The good, the pure, the beautiful,
> From graven stone and written scroll,
> From the old flower-fields of the soul,
> And, weary seekers for the best,
> We come back laden from our quest,

To find that all the sages said
Is in the Book our mothers read.

— John Greenleaf Whittier

Prayer: Our Father, today open our minds to the Spirit of God that he may reveal to us the wonders of our world. May he reveal the glory of thy love and the truth that is everlasting. We ask in the name of Jesus. Amen.

Life's Essential Compass

"Thy statutes have been my songs in the house of my pilgrimage." — Psalm 119:54

Some sailors were deserting their wrecked ship. They were all in the lifeboats and pushing away from the ship when one of them thought of something.

"Did anyone get the compass?" he called. The word went from lifeboat to lifeboat.

"No. No compass!"

What could they do on these little traveled waters without a compass?

"I will swim back and try to get it before the ship goes down," a brave man called.

So, at much risk to his own life he went back to the ship and sought the compass. When at last he returned with it safely to his companions there was much rejoicing.

"We will all be saved if we stay close together and are guided by the compass."

If we carry the Bible as our companion and guide we will be safe from the winds and storms of this world.

> "Run, run, and work," the law commands,
> But gives me neither feet nor hands;
> But sweeter sounds the gospel brings,
> It bids me fly, and gives me wings.

Prayer: Our Father, we thank thee for the privilege of walking with thee. May we ever take thee as our traveling companion. We ask in Jesus' name. Amen.

Someone Else's Pain

"He shall cover thee with his feathers, and under his wings shalt thou trust: his truth shall be thy shield and buckler. Thou shalt not be afraid for the terror by night; nor for the arrow that flieth by day." — Psalm 91:4, 5

Little Mellie was the baby of a large family. She often tried to imitate her older sisters. One day she watched as they took hot bread out of the oven. When their backs were turned she tried to open the oven door and was badly burned on her arm.

The sisters and brothers all felt bad because of her pain. Every day until she was better they doctored and petted her. Seeing their concern one day she said, "You hurt because I hurt."

When we are hurt we need only call upon our Father in heaven to heal and restore us.

> We never know another's pain
> We only feel our own.
> We never know real loneliness
> Until we're left alone.
>
> Too oft, it seems, our real concern
> Is just our selfish gain,
> And so we often shut our eyes
> To someone else's pain.
> — E. Jay Ritter

Prayer: Father, help us to follow Christ's example and be aware of the pain and need of those about us. We ask in the name of our Lord Jesus Christ. Amen.

The Pure Life

"Keep your heart with all vigilance; for from it flow the springs of life." — Proverbs 4:23

Jesus faced an impure world and yet he lived a perfect life. We are not divine so we cannot be perfect, yet we can take some of the same precautions Jesus took and make our lives purer.

One of the first rules for a pure life is to flee from temptation. Do not go where temptation is and say, "I will resist it." No, run away from it. Look up II Timothy 2:22 and see what Paul told young Timothy to do.

Talk about good things: the laws in the Bible, the love of God for sinners, memorize Bible verses. Jesus quoted some verses when he was tempted.

Avoid bad companions and do not read trashy literature.

Then last, but most important, if you would have a clean life, love God supremely and determine to serve him.

> Not bubbling waters to the thirsty swain,
> Not rest to weary laborers, faint with pain,

Not showers to larks, not sunshine to the bee,
Are half so precious as thy love to me —
  My Saviour.

Prayer: O Lord Jesus Christ, we humbly beseech thee, open our eyes to evil about us and help us with thy power to lead clean, pure lives. We pray in the name of Jesus our Lord. Amen.

What Do You Seek?

"And Jesus stood still, and commanded him to be called. And they called the blind man, saying unto him, be of good comfort, rise; he calleth thee." — Mark 10:49

One of the greatest things about America is that people may seek for better ways of life and find them.

Joseph Pulitzer left his home in Hungary and crossed to the United States when he was a boy of seventeen. He joined the cavalry of the North during the war between the states.

For a number of years Joseph did well just to have food to eat and a place to sleep. But he never minded hard work, and after he was released from the army he started to write and work as a reporter. He had as his motto, Accuracy and Service. He became very wealthy and though he has been dead many years his money still is serving others by way of the Pulitzer Prizes. What did he seek? To help others!

Almost any person can be judged by what they seek in life.

Sad one in secret bending low,
A dart in thy breast that the world may not know,
Striving the favor of God to win,
Asking his pardon for days of sin;
Press on, press on, with thy earnest cry,
"Jesus of Nazareth passeth by."

— Mrs. Sigourney

Prayer: Great God, our Father, who hast taught us that they who mourn shall be comforted; may we turn to thee in our sin and sorrow. We ask for Jesus name. Amen.

The Shepherding of God

The Lord is my shepherd;
  I shall not want.
He maketh me to lie down in green pastures:

He leadeth me beside the still waters.
He restoreth my soul:
   He leadeth me in the paths of righteousness
For His name's sake.

Yea though I walk through the valley
Of the shadow of death,
   I will fear no evil:
For thou art with me;
   Thy rod and thy staff they comfort me.

Thou preparest a table before me
   In the presence of mine enemies:
Thou anointest my head with oil;
   My cup runneth over.

Surely goodness and mercy shall
   Follow me all the days of my life:
And I will dwell in the house
   Of the Lord forever.

— Psalm 23:1-6

"This peaceful idyl (the twenty-third psalm) is a voice out of the maturer life of the psalmist, out of memories of care and battle and treachery; a voice that tells that peace and rest of heart depend not upon the absence of life's burdens, nor on the presence of nature's tranquilizing scenes, but solely upon the shepherding of God." (Marvin R. Vincent)

Prayer: Dear Father, shepherd of all mankind, help us to trust in thee. Give us courage and strength for the dangers of the world. We pray in the name of Jesus. Amen.

Knowing No Fear

"Come unto me, all ye that labor and are heavy laden, and I will give you rest. Take my yoke upon you, and learn of me; for I am meek and lowly in heart: and ye shall find rest unto your souls. For my yoke is easy and my burden is light."
— Matthew 11:28, 29, 30

A family went out in a boat for a summer outing. Soon a strong wind came up. They all became frightened, except the baby. The baby slept through all the frightening hour they were trying to get back to shore. The baby was clasped tight to her mother's breast and she knew no fear.

As Christians we should trust in our Saviour and know no fear when the storms of life assail us.

As those that watch for the day,
  Through the restless night of pain,
When the first faint streaks of gray
  Bring rest and ease again —
As they turn their sleepless eyes
  The Eastern sky to see,
Long hours before sunrise —
  So waiteth my soul for Thee!

Prayer: Our Father, may we ever know that thou art the protector of all who put their trust in thee. May we praise thy Holy name and honor thee with our lives. We ask in the name of Jesus. Amen.

Love and Joy

"And now abideth faith, hope, love, these three; but the greatest of these is love." — I Corinthians 13:13

If I knew the box where the smiles are kept,
  No matter how large the key
Or strong the bolt, I would try so hard
  'Twould open, I know for me.

Then over the land and sea broadcast
  I'd scatter the smiles to play,
That the children's faces might hold them fast
  For many and many a day.

If I knew a box that was large enough
  To hold all the frowns I meet,
I would try to gather them, every one,
  From nursery school and street,

Then, folding and holding, I'd pack them in
  And turn the monster key;
I'd hire a giant to drop the box
  To the depths of the deep, deep sea.

What is the source of joy for people? Is it love for family, work, home, pleasure, travel? We could write pages and not name all the things people seek after as a source of joy. Yet without the love of Jesus all joy is at best very fleeting. On the other hand if we have the love of Christ in our hearts it helps us to find joy in all other things. Christ's love makes us content with our family, our work and our friends.

61

Prayer: Our Father, we long for a closer walk with thee. We know if we have thy love in our hearts we will understand each other better. We will seek to bear one another's burdens. Grant us this love in the name of Jesus. Amen.

Seeking Lost Sheep

"What man of you, having an hundred sheep, if he lose one of them, does not leave the ninety and nine in the wilderness, and go after that which is lost, until he find it? And when he cometh home, he calleth together his friends and neighbors, saying unto them, Rejoice with me; for I have found my sheep which was lost." — Luke 15:4, 6

In this story Jesus showed how active and energetic his love for his children is. His was not a religion of mere talk and sentiment, it was a religion of action.

He went in search of the lost sheep — not for just a little while but until it was found.

When Jesus found the lost sheep he brought it home. We have but to look in almost any direction to find people who are lost from God and need to be brought home. Are we seeking to bring them into the fold?

When the sheep was safely back in the fold there was great rejoicing!

> Hark 'tis the Shepherd's voice I hear,
> Out in the desert dark and drear,
> Calling the sheep who've gone astray
> Far from the Shepherd's fold away.

> — Alex Thomas

Prayer: Father, put it in our hearts to go out and seek for the lost around us. We pray in the name of the great Shepherd. Amen.

The Dinner Guest

"But they constrained him, saying, Abide with us: for it is toward evening, and the day is far spent. And he went in to tarry with them." — Luke 24:29

> Suppose they had not asked him in,
> Inviting him to share
> The comfort of their fireside and
> Their simple evening fare.

That intimate companionship
Enabled them to find
A wonder and divinity
To which they had been blind.

For as he blessed and broke the bread
They saw the commonplace
Akin, somehow, to holiness
And touched by heavenly grace.

So it has always been that hearts
Have learned to know Christ best,
When he has been invited in —
A loved and honored guest.

As we travel life's pathway how often do we invite Jesus in to sup with us?

Prayer: Dear Lord, bless us with thy presence at our table. May our ears be open to hear thy word. For Jesus' sake. Amen.

The Need for Considerate Hearts

"Whom have I in heaven but thee? and there is none upon earth that I desire beside thee." — Psalm 73:25

Carelessness and lack of proper consideration are responsible for a large part of the sorrow in the world. Sometimes we are caught in a current and are swept along without giving proper consideration to our deeds. We could stop much of the rough grinding of the cogs of life if we just used oil of consideration for those about us.

A door can be a boon, for it can keep intruders out,
And it can be a comfort when bad weather is about;
But let us not forget that it can also bar the way
To kindly folk who'd drop in, just to pass the time of day.

If we are too much sheltered by the heavy lock and key,
Then we are apt to find out just how lonely we can be;
For heartaches soon vanish, and new happiness begins,
Through the open door that's waiting for a friend to enter in.

— Anne Hayward

Prayer: Our Father, give us considerate hearts for those about us. Give us eyes of love to see those in need of extra kindness and consideration. We ask in Jesus' name. Amen.

Bitterness and Peace

"Behold, for peace I had great bitterness: but thou hast in love to my soul delivered it from the pit of corruption: for thou hast cast all my sins behind thy back." — Isaiah 38:17

Are we ever bitter over our sins? We should be. We should never be satisfied with our sinful condition.

God loves us no matter how deep in the pit of sin we sink, if we only seek his help and show that we want to repent.

Two singers were very jealous of each other. Only hate seemed to live in them. Then one grew very ill and could not work. Soon she had no money for doctors and medicine. Her rival decided to help. He announced a benefit concert for the stricken one. The concert was a great success and he brought the money to her. The hate within her heart melted away. She had seen a glimpse of true Christian character.

> Lord, give me eyes that I may see
> The glance of those who look to me
> To help them in their time of need.
> Lord, give me eyes that I may heed.
> Lord give me ears that I may hear·
> The voice of service calling clear —
> Service to those not blest as I;
> Lord, give me ears to hear their cry.
>
> — Warren M. Baker

Prayer: Our Father, take all bitterness away from our hearts. Cast our sins behind thy back and make us worthy of thy love. We ask in Jesus' name. Amen.

God's Golden Rule

"Therefore all things whatsoever ye would that men should do to you, do ye even so to them: for this is the law and the prophets." — Matthew 7:12

Do not expect from others more than you are willing to do for them. Be willing to do for others all you would like from them under the same circumstances. The golden rule is a reasonable and wholesome principle.

Little Billy had a bad habit, biting other children in the nursery school. His teachers tried several forms of punishment but Billy kept on biting the other children.

One day little Mary's mother said to her, "If Billy starts to bite you, you bite him good and hard."

Sure enough in a day or two Billy grabbed Mary's hand and started to bite. Mary gave him such a hard bite on his arm he was never known to bite again.

> I think that good must come of good,
>   And ill of evil — surely unto all
> In every place of time, seeing sweet fruit
> Groweth from wholesome roots or bitter things
> From poison stocks; yea, seeing, too, how spite
> Breeds hate — and kindness friends — or patience
> Peace.

— Edwin Arnold

Prayer: Father let thy spirit come upon us in such a way that we will always seek to live by the Golden Rule. Help our deeds to be acceptable in thy sight. We ask for Jesus' sake. Amen.

All for God's Honor and Glory

"Humble yourselves in the sight of the Lord, and he shall lift you up." — James 4:10

Pride in a job well done is fine. But we should remember that without God's blessing it would be for naught. Everything man is and does is from God. The glory and honor should be his and his alone.

> Before Elisha's gate
> The Syrian leper stood
> But could not brook to wait,
> He deemed himself too good:
> He thought the prophet would attend
> And not to *him* a message send.
>
> Have I this journey come,
> And will he not be seen?
> I were as well at home,
> Would washing make me clean;
> Why must I wash in Jordan's flood?
> Damascus rivers are as good.
>
> Thus by his foolish pride
> He almost missed a cure;
> Howe'er at length he tried,
> And found the method sure:
> Soon as the pride was brought to yield,
> The leprosy was quickly healed.

— John Newton

Prayer: Heavenly Father, may we always do our work well, never forgetting to give thee the glory. In Jesus' name we pray. Amen.

Trusting God Alone

"Then Paul stood in the midst of Mars' hill, and said, Ye men of Athens, I perceive that in all things ye are too superstitious."
— Acts 17:22

Paul was preaching to the most superstitious people in his day. Today the word superstitious describes people who will not walk under a ladder or who will not sleep in room 13, or many others.

I remember well one day I was going to town in a hurry and a black cat crossed my path. In spite of myself, just for a moment, an old, childish whim came to me and I thought, "You will have bad luck if you don't turn around."

How foolish for Christian people to think that anyone save God can control our fate.

> All is of God! If He but wave His hand,
> The mists collect, the rain falls thick and loud,
> Till, with a smile of light on sea and land,
> Lo! He looks back from the departing cloud.
> Angels of life and death alike are His;
> Without His leave they pass no threshold o'er;
> Who then would wish or dare, believing this,
> Against His messengers to shut the door?

— J. R. Lowell

Prayer: Our most gracious Father help us to always trust in thee only. Make us good servants of thine. We pray in the name of Jesus. Amen.

The Need for a Forgiving Heart

"For if ye forgive men their trespasses, your heavenly Father will also forgive you." — Matthew 6:14

Asking forgiveness is hard for most of us. Sometimes forgiving is even harder. The wrong spirit about little things can hurt us, and often hurt the other fellow.

When we think about how much God has to forgive us for we certainly should be willing to forgive others.

> Oh, it's just the little homely things,
> The unobtrusive, friendly things,

The "won't-you-let-me-help-you" things
    That make our pathway light.
And it's just the jolly joking things,
The "never-mind-the-trouble" things,
The "laugh-with-me-it's-funny" things,
    That make the world seem bright.
For all the countless famous things,
The wondrous record-breaking things
Those never-can-be-equalled things,
    That all the papers cite,
Are not like little human things,
The every-day-encounter things,
The "just-because-I-like-you" things,
    That make us happy quite.
So here's to all the little things,
The done-and-then-forgotten things,
The "oh, it's — simply-nothing" things,
    That make life worth the fight.

Prayer: Father, today give us a forgiving heart. Give us the heart to help others by doing the little things that make life sweeter. We pray in the name of Jesus. Amen.

Watch Your Words

"By your words you will be justified, and by your words you will be condemned." — Matthew 12:37

In the ninth commandment (Exodus 20:16) we read, "You shall not bear false witness against your neighbor."

The problems caused by people bearing false witness are many and very harmful. The problems hurt three persons: the one bearing false witness, the one to whom he speaks, and the one about whom he speaks. The verse in Matthew tells us we will be justified or condemned by our words; so we should be extra careful what we say.

If we think someone is telling a story about a friend or acquaintance we should walk away and not listen.

So many kinds of lies there be,
So many ways to lie,
So many tongues hung loose and free
To twist the truth awry.

Despised as liars always are,
God rates as worst the kind

Whose lies are half-truth, stretched so far
All truth is left behind.

Prayer: Dear Father may we resolve today to be truthful in all things. Help us to be wise and considerate of other people and never say unkind things about others. We ask in the name of one who was always kind and pure, Jesus our Saviour. Amen.

Christian Graces

"But as for you, man of God, shun all this; aim at righteousness, godliness, faith, love, steadfastness, gentleness."

— I Timothy 6:11

When you read the words, *Christian Graces,* do they paint a picture of the best Christian you know? Do you picture someone like the person described in the verse above? I do.

A mother I knew thought her daughter must take dancing lessons. "Why?" I asked her.

"Oh, so she will grow up to be more graceful."

That same mother who was so eager for her daughter to have a graceful body, never once took time to see that she was brought up to know the Christian Graces and practice them. Many daughters in Christian homes may not be so graceful, I suppose, but most of them grow up to be good Christian women and work for their churches and communities. God's promise still holds, "Train up a child in the way he should go, and when he is old he will not depart therefrom" (Proverbs 22:6).

God might have used His sunset gold so sparingly
He might have doled His blossoms out quite grudgingly;
He might have put one wee star in the sky
But since He gave so lavishly,
Why should not I?

Prayer: Father, in these days of stress may we ever put Christ as the center of our lives, for in his name we pray. Amen.

Church Attendance

"I was glad when they said unto me, let us go into the house of the Lord." — Psalm 122:1

God bless all those whose membership is here,
Thy people, Lord, who love Thy house and Thee.

God bless the strangers gathered in our midst;
Lonely, perhaps, and far from home they need
The blessed comfort of their Father's house,
The proffered bread of life on which to feed.
God bless the one who here propounds Thy truths,
Be in his heart, speak through the words he speaks
That every listening, eager one may find
The wisdom and the comfort that he seeks.
 And when at last, the benediction said.
 May we go, strengthened for the days ahead.

In the church I attend the children are kept in the nursery until they are four years old. All through the last year, before they promote from the nursery, they are told about the "big church." They are taken on walking tours of the sanctuary and told about the organ and the choir and other things. When they are old enough to attend "big church" they are well prepared for it. They look forward to their first Sunday there. They learn to love the services.

All true Christians like to attend the services in their church. If they do not, they should examine their hearts and see what is wrong.

Prayer: Father, make us appreciate the privilege of attending services in thy visible church. We pray in Jesus name. Amen.

Sowing Good Seeds

"They sow the wind, and they shall reap the whirlwind."

— Hosea 8:7

We should stop periodically and look at our sowing. Are we sowing the whirlwind? What are we sowing in the lives of our children, our pupils, or our friends? Remember we will reap what we sow.

Children imitate their elders. So much of their learning comes from watching someone else and doing likewise. Are we sowing good seeds in the things we say and do?

As for friends, are we "sowing seeds of kindness"?

 Are we sowing seeds of goodness?
  They shall blossom bright ere long.
 Are we sowing seeds of discord?
  They shall ripen into wrong.
 Are we sowing seeds of honor?

They shall bring forth golden grain.
Are we sowing seeds of falsehood?
We shall yet reap bitter pain.
Whatsoe'er our sowing be,
Reaping, we its fruit must see.

We can never be too careful
What the seed our hands shall sow;
Love from love is sure to ripen,
Hate from hate is sure to grow.
Seeds of good or ill we scatter
Heedlessly along our way;
But a glad or grievous fruitage
Waits us at the harvest day.

Prayer: Dear Lord, may we be ever watchful of the words we speak and the things we do. May our influence be for good and not for evil. In Jesus' name we pray. Amen.

Rule or Ruin?

"But as many as received him, to them gave he power to become the sons of God, even to them that believe on his name."
— John 1:12

Many people have failed to achieve the best they could in life because they were too full of false pride. They wanted, as the old saying goes, "to rule or ruin."

Nancy was just such a girl. She was pretty and popular. A new girl moved to town who was prettier, and quickly became more popular. From that time forward life in that small town seemed to be a tug-of-war between the two girls for power. Whatever one wanted the other was sure to want it more and try to get it. So both became less and less popular and spent the remainder of their lives trying to out-do each other.

The haughty feet of power shall fail
Where meekness surely goes;
No cunning finds the key of heaven,
No strength its gates unclose.
Alone to guilelessness and love
Those gates shall open fall:
The mind of pride is nothingness,
The childlike heart is all.

Prayer: Most loving, heavenly Father, help us today to be sweet and gentle. May we be humble servants, willing to serve thee in this world. We pray in the name of one who had all power on earth and in heaven. Amen.

An Answered Prayer

"But Jesus said, Forbid him not: for there is no man which shall do a miracle in my name, that can lightly speak evil of me."
— Mark 9:39

Many years ago our phone rang in the early morning hours. Answering I heard my father's voice, "Baby sister is dying; hurry home if you want to see her." Gathering up a few clothes for our own small daughter we hastily set out on a sad journey.

My sister was dying from a disease the doctors called colitis. Five of the doctors in the small town where my parents lived had told them, "No hope."

After we arrived and looked at the wasted, little body, we had no hope either. A nurse, a friend of my mother, came and she and mother started feeding the baby spoonfuls of beaten egg-white. All day long they fed her all she would take. Next day she was much better. The doctors all said, "It is a miracle."

The nurse said "It is the egg-white."

We knew it was the hand of God.

Months later after the child was able to run and play again, my parents heard of a few friends who had met and prayed until far into the night for her, the night she was supposed to die. It was, indeed, an answer to prayer.

Prayer: Help us to pray in faith relying on thy promises. For Christ's sake. Amen.

He Still Leads

"I will smite them with the pestilence, and disinherit them, and will make of thee a greater nation and mightier than they."
— Numbers 14:12

God took the Israelites from Egypt as poor, ignorant slaves. They had not traveled beyond the villages where they had been forced to labor each day; they had not been to schools and learned of the things of the world; yet he made of them a great nation.

"Unexplained as it was in the world, and without parallel in any other nation, it shows that there was some peculiar power at work in the Jewish dispensation, and that the people had been under a special, educating Providence."

Even today God looks after those who believe and trust in him. He still leads and directs his followers.

An infidel, Dryden, says of the Bible:

> Whence but from heaven, could men unskilled in arts,
> In several ages born, in several parts,
> Weave such agreeing truths? or how or why,
> Should all conspire to cheat us with a lie?
> Unasked their pains, ungrateful their advice,
> Starving their gain and martyrdom their price.

Prayer: Our most powerful and mighty God, help us as a nation to trust in thee. Help us as individuals to know there is no power greater than thine. Make us true servants of thine. We pray in Jesus' name. Amen.

Two Worlds

"And we have borne the image of the earthy, we shall also bear the image of the heavenly." — I Corinthians 15:49

When we hear people talking about going to other planets, many of us are tempted to say, "One world is enough for me."

If we read the Easter story closely we see that there are people living in two worlds — the world of heavenly things and the world of earthly things. The heavenly will eventually be victorious over death and trouble.

Everyone has some interest in immortality. Christians feel secure in their belief; unbelievers feel a sense of frustration and often defeat.

> 'Tis Revelation satisfies all doubts,
> Explains all mysteries except her own,
> And so illumines the path of life,
> That fools discover it and stray no more.
>
> What glory gilds the sacred page!
> Majestic! Like the sun,
> It gives a light to every age;
> It gives, but borrows none.
>
> Most wondrous book! bright candle of the Lord!
> Star of eternity! the only star
> By which the bark of man could navigate
> The sea of life, and gain the coast of bliss securely.

Prayer: Father, help us to know we are only here to salute the world as we pass by. We are going in the direction of a different world; a world where there is no sorrow or crying. We ask in the name of Jesus. Amen.

Watch What You Say

"Sayest thou this thing of thyself or did others tell it thee?"
— John 18:34

Jesus was speaking to Pilate. Pilate had to answer that he had heard what he had spoken from the Jews.

How many times we hurt others and ourselves by repeating what we have merely heard. Did you ever play gossip? Someone starts a sentence at the beginning of the circle and it is whispered all around. When it comes back to the original person it sounds quite different.

> If we knew the cares and crosses
> Crowding 'round our neighbor's way.
> If we knew of all his losses
> Sorely grievous day by day;
> Would we then so often chide him
> Casting o'er his life a shadow
> Leaving on his heart a stain?
> Let us reach into our bosoms
> For the key to other lives,
> And with love to erring nature,
> Cherish good that still survives;
> So that when our disrobed spirits
> Soar to realms of light again,
> We may say, dear Father, judge us
> As we judged our fellow men.

Prayer: O Lord, make us to walk with thee here in such a way that we will not speak ill of our friends and neighbors. We ask in Jesus name. Amen.

Too Busy *Not* to Pray

". . . in everything by prayer and supplication, let your requests be made known unto God." — Philippians 4:6

We all have heard of people who say they are too busy to pray. Recently I heard of a woman who said she was too busy not to pray. I believe she had a point.

Prayer does not interrupt your time, activities, or life; it is the business of talking things over as we go along with a companion. In life we face questions each day. What? How? When? Where? Only God can answer all of these.

Go when the morning shineth,
   Go when the noon is bright
Go when the eve declineth,
   Go in the hush of night:
Go with pure mind and feeling,
   Fling every fear away,
And in thy chamber kneeling,
   Do thou in secret pray.

Or if 'tis e'er denied thee
   In solitude to pray,
Should holy thoughts come o'er thee
   When friends are round thy way,
E'en then the silent breathing
   Of thy spirit raised above,
May reach His throne of glory,
   Who is mercy, truth, and love.

           — John Cress Bell

Prayer: O Lord, gather thy sheep and lambs and carry them in thy bosom. Feed thy sheep for thou art the great shepherd. We ask in Christ's name. Amen.

A Great Household of Believers

"You are no longer strangers and sojourners, but you are fellow citizens with the saints and members of the household of God." — Ephesians 2:19

We all like to be with the majority when we can do so in good conscience. Do you ever feel that you are the only Christian? You are not. There are millions more. We belong to a great household of believers.

My mother said that in the early twentieth century most of the farm families wanted many children to help with the farming. Most farm homes had long tables with benches on each side. A husband and wife felt very fortunate if both benches were well filled.

As Christians we should feel a part of a great family. We should want to see that family grow larger and larger.

    He drew a circle and shut me out,
    Heretic, rebel, a thing to flout.
    But love and I had a wit to win;
    We drew a circle that took him in.

           — Edwin Markham

Prayer: Father, may we know and be glad that we are members of the household of God. Help us to conduct our lives as children of Thine should. We pray in the name of Jesus. Amen.

The Light of His Way

"If we walk in the light, as he is in the light, we have fellowship with one another, and the blood of Jesus his Son cleanses us from all sin." — I John 1:7

The man who knows and understands Jesus is the man who walks in the light of his love. If we love Christ and are loyal to him we grow in knowledge and his truth is revealed to us.

In our family there is a blind lady. She has not always been blind and her trouble came on gradually. It fascinated the children when she would reach for something on the cabinet, or table. She would feel very gently. Then when her hand touched the object she would confidently pick it up. If we know Christ we should not grope but be confident as we walk in the light of his way.

> Dream not too much of what you'll do tomorrow,
> How well you'll work perhaps another year;
> Tomorrow's chance you do not need to borrow
> Today is here.
>
> Boast not too much of mountains you will master,
> The while you linger in the vale below;
> To dream is well, but plodding brings us faster —
> To where we go.
>
> Swear not some day to break some habit's fetter,
> When this old year is dead and passed away;
> If you have need of living better, wiser,
> Begin today!

Prayer: Lord, help us to see thee better. Amen.

God's Errand

"The Spirit of the Lord is upon me, because he hath anointed me to preach the gospel to the poor; he hath sent me to heal the broken-hearted, to preach deliverance to the captives, and recovering of sight to the blind, to set at liberty them that are bruised." — Luke 4:18, 19

When I was a little girl my mother sent me on an errand. My baby sister was seriously ill. I had to walk sixteen blocks to town and get some medicine prescribed by the doctor. I loved my sister very much and I returned home as rapidly as possible. My sister was soon resting well.

The Lord sends us on an errand too. The world is desperately sick. God asks us to bring the good tidings that there is a remedy for the world's ills. May the Spirit of the Lord make us willing and able to carry out his mandate.

> We've a story to tell to the nations,
> That shall turn their hearts to the right,
> A story of truth and sweetness,
> A story of peace and light.
>
> For the darkness shall turn to dawning,
> And the dawning to noonday bright,
> And Christ's great kingdom shall come on earth,
> The kingdom of love and light.

Prayer: Father, may we feel thy call to us. May we answer thy commission and serve thee aright. We pray in Jesus' name. Amen.

My Father's World

"The earth is the Lord's and the fulness thereof, the world and those who dwell therein." — Psalm 24:1

Isn't it wonderful to know that the universe belongs to God. What a sad thing it would be for us if the universe belonged to a landlord who would not wait past the first of the month for the rent. We all owe so much and are so slow with our payments.

Some people went off the deep end and tried to make the world believe God was dead. How foolish! I know he lives because I feel him in my own heart. I know he lives because he patiently waits for us to turn to him and trust. If God turned the world over to the devil for just a moment chaos would destroy us.

> This is my Father's world,
> And to my listening ears,
> All nature sings, and round me rings;
> The music of the spheres.
>
> This is my Father's world
> I rest me in the thought,
> Of rocks and trees, of skies and seas;
> His hands the wonders wrought.

Prayer: Our God, whose greatness is revealed in all creation, we thank thee for our world so great. We thank thee for letting us live in such a marvelous age. Make us worthy of thy many blessings. We pray in the name of Jesus. Amen.

The Believer's Life

"Mine age is departed, and is removed from me as a shepherd's tent: I have cut off like a weaver my life; he will cut me off with pining sickness; from day even to night wilt thou make an end of me." — Isaiah 38:12

The life of the believer should be interesting. Have you ever been walking in the woods in the fall of the year? As one goes along there are so many interesting things to see. There are nuts to be picked up and bright colored leaves to gather.

The believer who is not finding his walk with God interesting is not looking about at life and taking a part in it.

The life we live will show to those about us in what we believe. If we walk with God it shows. Men may doubt what you say but they will believe what you live.

If we do not have the life of God dwelling within us, we are constantly growing more selfish and ugly. If Christ dwells within we grow more like him each day.

Life is uncertain, we must make the most of each day.

> True religion is more than doctrine,
> Something must be known and felt.

Prayer: Heavenly Father, may our conduct today contribute to thy glory and to our spiritual life and welfare. We ask in the name of Jesus. Amen.

Life's Trials

"The heart of the prudent getteth knowledge; and the ear of the wise seeketh knowledge." — Proverbs 18:15

We like to remember Columbus because we think of him as being the one who discovered our country. He had no idea how large the world was, how round it was, or how far the ocean stretched but he was willing to seek and discover.

> It isn't the work that tries us, but the sights we have to see;
> The children bowing to idols, the slaves who cannot be free,
> With those who of evil spirit spend all their lives in fear,
> And women toiling in bondage, no hope of heaven to cheer.

It isn't the work that wears us; at least, not what we do,
But that which is left undone when our busy day is through;
It's turning away the scholars who want our schools to share,
And saying "No" to the people who beg for a teacher's care.

It isn't the work that kills us; but the strange, indifferent life
Of those who, too, are Christians, but stand aloof from strife;
It's keeping up the struggle that we abroad must live
Without the friendly backing which you at home could give.

— By a Missionary

Prayer: Father, if we are not willing to go to other lands, make us willing to hold the ropes in order that others may carry the Word. We pray in Jesus' name. Amen.

Deliver Us from Judgment

"The law of the Lord is perfect, converting the soul: the testimony of the Lord is sure, making wise the simple."

— Psalm 19:7

In recent years we have heard much talk about the laws of our land often seeming to protect the criminal. We read and hear of cases that seem in our eyes to be unfair and unjust to the victim of wrong. God's law is perfect. We cannot hope to keep it without the help of Jesus Christ.

When some fellow yields to temptation
And breaks a conventional law,
We look for no good in his make-up
But oh! how we look for the flaw!

No one will ask, "How tempted?"
Nor allow for the battles he fought;
His name becomes food for the jackals —
For us who have never been caught.

"He's sinned!" shout we from the housetops;
We forget the good he has done;
We center on one lost battle
And forget the times he has won.

"Come; gaze on the sinner!" we thunder,
"And by his example be taught
That his footsteps lead to destruction,"
Cry we who have never been caught.

I'm a sinner, O Lord, and I know it;
I'm weak and I blunder and fail;
I'm tossed on life's stormy ocean
Like ships embroiled in a gale.

I'm willing to trust in Thy mercy,
To keep the commandments Thou'st taught;
But deliver me, Lord, from the judgment
Of the "saints" who have never been caught.

Prayer: Father, keep us from being unkind in our judgment of others. We ask in Jesus' name. Amen.

God Is Counting on You

"The fame of him went out into every place of the country round about." — Luke 4:37

Lillian is not famous outside her own community but mention her name in her own town and people will say, "Oh, yes, I know her." She is not young and beautiful, nor is she rich in worldly goods. Lillian is a Christian. During an epidemic when she was just a young bride she went from house to house taking care of the sick. She paid people's bills and ran their errands; took care of the children. All the years since people have kept calling on her for help. The youth has left her face, her body is older and more frail, but she is known as a good woman.

No matter what others are doing, my friend,
Or what they are leaving undone,
God's counting on you to keep on with the job
'Till the very last battle is won.
He's counting on you to be faithful:
He's counting on you to be true.
Yes, others may work, or others may shirk,
But remember — God's counting on you.

Prayer: O God, make thyself known to us, show us the works Thou would'st have us to do. Bow our wills to thine, yield our spirits to the influence of the Holy Spirit. We pray in the name of Jesus. Amen.

If We Only Understood

"He said, Abba, Father, all things are possible unto thee; take away this cup from me: nevertheless not what I will, but what thou wilt." — Mark 14:36

One time we were visiting in the country. Two boys in the home had caught some birds and had cages built for them. The owl just sat in his cage and blinked. He was content with his lot. Not so the young eagle. He beat against the wire with his wings and pecked with his beak. He wanted freedom and in a few days would have beat himself to death trying to break the bondage. The boys being gentle fellows turned the young eagle loose and he was soon away in the woods.

> Oft we judge each other harshly
>   Knowing not life's hidden force,
> Knowing not the fount of action
>   Is less turbid at its source,
>
> Seeing not amid the evil
>   All the golden grains of good,
> Oh, we'd love each other better
>   If we only understood.
>
> Could we but draw the curtain
>   That surrounds each other's lives,
> See the naked heart and spirit
>   Know what impulse, the action gives,
> Often we should find it better,
>   Purer than we judged we should,
> We would love each other better
>   If we only understood.

Prayer: Almighty God, our Father in Heaven, we appreciate the freedom from sin thou hast provided for us through Christ Jesus. Make us worthy of thy love. We ask in Jesus' name. Amen.

Real Christmas Gifts

The shepherds were afraid the night they heard the angels sing, but the sheep and the flocks and herds were quiet. They were trusting in the same shepherd as always, and saw no change. Herod was afraid. He saw not a tiny babe in a manger but pictured a king who would take his place. He heard not a song of joy but only felt hate.

The tidings were brought to all people but only a few heard.

> I dreamed I saw Christ come again
> Across the snowy Christmas plain,
> With gifts and blessings in His hand
> For every heart in every land;

But he brought not a painted toy,
Some little superficial joy,
A dole a moment's need to cure,
A Christmas dinner for the poor.

He brought to all men everywhere
The right to do, the right to share,
The right to think, the right to learn,
The right to labor and to earn,
Courage to walk with head erect.
In peace of mind and self-respect.
The right to face life unafraid.
Oh, what a Christmas Day it made.

— Ilion T. Jones

Prayer: Father, we are filled with tender memories on this eve of our Saviour's birth. We ask that you will fill our hearts with the presence of the King of kings. Give us generous hearts and may the star shine brightly and the angels sing more beautifully today because our hearts are right. In his name. Amen.

Laws to Help Us

"And in those days there was no king in Israel: every man did that which was right in his own eyes." — Judges 21:25

What a world we would live in if every man went by his own law. No one would be safe for a moment from the ones who feel it is safe to rob and kill. We would be in a state of utter confusion.

God knowing our condition gave us laws to abide by and lawmakers to enforce them.

I was the oldest child in my family. Often my mother would entrust me with the care of my younger brother and sister. When she left she would say, "Now you mind Amy until I return."

God left us a world that is not perfect and our laws are often disappointing in the way they are enforced but one day he will return. If the laws have not been kept he will make a perfect judgment.

My soul is but the battle ground between the base and pure:
What though today I sound sin's depths its miseries endure,
And walk down the valley way of sorrow and despair
With want as my companion and hand in hand with care,

Tomorrow I will climb the heights that lead to realms above,
And comprehend the mystery of Life . . . of Death . . . of
Love.

— Jeanne Breton

Prayer: Father, give us the love in our hearts to obey thy laws.
We pray in the name of Christ. Amen.

Children of the King

"Are you not behaving like ordinary men?"

— I Corinthians 3:3 (Moffatt translation)

"We are children of the minister, so we can't act like
that." How often as a child I have said this or had my mother
say it to me.

Our own pastor's little girl was near a boy at a ball game
when he said an ugly word.

"You shouldn't say that," she said to him.

"Who are you?" he asked her.

"I'm a preacher's kid," she replied proudly.

"Oh, I'm sorry. I will not say that again," said the boy. He
was on his best behavior the rest of the ball game.

As Christians we are children of a King. We should always
remember this and act accordingly.

> The little birds that fly in air;
> The sheep that need the shepherd's care;
> The pearls that deep in ocean lie;
> The gold that charms the miser's eye;
> All from his lips some truth proclaim,
> Or learn to tell their Maker's name.

Prayer: Lord, make us ever proud to own thee as our Maker,
our Lord, and King. Keep us from acting like ordinary men. We
pray in the name of the one who was of all men most extraordinary. Amen.

Living for God or the World

*"And Elijah came unto all the people and said: How long
halt ye between two opinions? If the Lord be God, follow Him,
but if Baal, then follow him."* — I Kings 18:21

We face questions every day, Where is our life going? What
purpose do we have in life? Will we live for God or for the
world?

How we face these questions determines whether we will be happy or disgruntled, whether we will be useful or just a wasted piece of driftwood on the sea of life.

> Work hard today and pray,
> Be resolute and say,
> "I will not fail in work of mine
> Though I must toil till bright stars shine
> And midnight falls."
>
> Tomorrow when the sun
> Shines on thy duty done,
> Thou wilt rejoice and gladly sing;
> To thee thy task sweet peace will bring
> And rest complete.
>
> And finished work abides,
> Thy toil doth crystallize
> The thoughts of brain, thine acts of will,
> Thy very life continuing still,
> Beyond life's span.
>
> — Charles E. Earle

Prayer: Dear Lord, we pour our hearts out to thee. We want our choice in life to be of service for thee. May we meditate daily on thy Word and will. May we lead others to make the right choices, also. We ask in Jesus' name. Amen.

Child Training

"Train up a child in the way he should go: and when he is old, he will not depart from it." — *Proverbs* 22:6

Sherri was expecting a new baby in her family. Her mother often talked to her about how she must be kind to the baby and that she would have to share her toys.

One day as they talked she said to her mother, "I will make it be a good baby."

Sometimes we are hungry for children and when God blesses us with them we forget to train them to be good. We indulge them in extravagances and whims and they do not grow up in the way they should.

> I took a piece of plastic clay
> And idly fashioned it one day,
> And as my fingers pressed it still
> It moved and yielded to my will.

83

I came again when days were past,
The bit of clay was hard at last
The form I gave it still it bore
And I could change that form no more.

I took a piece of living clay
And gently formed it day by day,
And molded with my power and art
A young child's soft and tender heart.

I came again when years were gone,
It was a man I looked upon,
He still that early impress bore,
And I could change him — nevermore.

Prayer: Give us a sense of responsibility as we train our children, we ask in Jesus' name. Amen.

A Mansion Awaits Us

"In my Father's house are many mansions: if it were not so, I would have told you. I go to prepare a place for you."

— John 14:2

To every hungry soul He gives from out His bounteous store
Its needs — its lessons — Who would ask for more?

How many times in life when things seemed scarce here on earth have I thought of the mansion my Lord is preparing for me. I have never thought of it in terms of beauty; just in terms of peace and quiet. Yet Jesus wants us as Christians to know an inner peace and tranquility here.

Promises are so nice when the one making the promise plans to keep that promise. Jesus is busy now getting that mansion ready for his children. We must get ready to occupy it.

Prayer:

Dear Lord! kind Lord!
Gracious Lord! I pray
Thou wilt look on all I love,
Tenderly to-day!
Weed their hearts of weariness;
Scatter every care
Down a wake of angel-wings
Winnowing the air.
Bring unto the sorrowing
All release from pain;

Let the lips of laughter
Overflow again;
And with all the needy
O divide, I pray,
This vast treasure of content
That is mine to-day!

— Riley

Longing for Jesus

"And it came to pass, that, when Jesus was returned, the people gladly received him: for they were all waiting for him."
— Luke 8:40

When I left home as a bride we moved to a distant city and I could not go back for three months. Those were such long months because I had never been away before — and I was homesick. My home looked like a mansion at the end of three months when I returned. My family all waited at the door for me and seemed glad to see me.

What a joy it must have been to Jesus to return from a country where the people begged him to leave, to a place where they welcomed him and waited his coming.

I have a longing in my heart for Jesus,
I have a longing in my heart for Him;
I have a longing just to see His face.
Although I know His presence lingers near me,

Longing, longing for Jesus,
I have a longing in my heart for Him;
Just to be near Him, to feel His presence,
I have a longing in my heart for Him.

I have a longing just to walk with Jesus,
I have a longing just to hold His hand:
To know He's there forever near to guide me,
To know His love will never let me go.

To you who do not know this man named Jesus,
You've never lived or found life's greatest joy;
Oh, won't you now take Him as Lord and Saviour,
And know the fullness of His matchless love.
— Richard D. Baker

Prayer: As we wait for the return of our dear Saviour may we seek to live for him each day. In his name we pray. Amen.

Listening to the Lord

"And she had a sister called Mary, which also sat at Jesus' feet, and heard his word." — Luke 10:39

When we think of sitting at someone's feet we think of listening to him as he speaks. We should always be listening for the words of Jesus. We should always listen with an attitude of worship and lowliness. When we sit at the feet of Jesus we must be aware of his love for us and we must ask him to take possession of our lives.

When we give ourselves over to sitting at Jesus' feet we find satisfaction and assurance in life.

> At the feet of Jesus, list'ning to His word;
> Learning wisdom's lesson from her loving Lord;
> Mary led by heavenly grace
> Chose the meek disciple's place.
> At the feet of Jesus is the place for me;
> There a humble learner would I choose to be.

Prayer: Father help us ever to sit humbly at thy feet and learn of thee. Make us meek and mild, and help us always to choose the better part of service. We pray in the name of our dear Saviour. Amen.

Christ's Blessed Invitation

"And when Jesus came to the place, he looked up, and saw him, and said unto him, Zacchaeus, make haste, and come down; for today I must abide at thy house." — Luke 19:5

Jesus invited himself to Zacchaeus' house because he had a gift for Zacchaeus. He had the gift of eternal life to bestow upon his new friend.

Jesus could see the good in Zacchaeus and he wanted to claim him for his own kingdom.

Several things worked together that day. God put it in the heart of Zacchaeus to want to see Jesus. He had to overcome the obstacle of being a short man, so he climbed a tree. Jesus, as he walked along, could feel a longing heart nearby. So he looked up into the tree and called to Zacchaeus.

I remember one time when I was a little girl and a girl in school told me she was going home with me. I felt so excited because she was a little older than I and we did not often play together. She invited herself but I was happy.

Prayer: Almighty God, our dear Father, we rejoice that you will come into our hearts and dwell with us. We are grateful for thy love. We pray in the name of Jesus. Amen.

Linked with God

"Then said Jesus, Father, forgive them; for they know not what they do." — Luke 23:34

Prayer is the greatest power we have on earth. What a pity this power is often used the least. When we pray we link ourselves with God who is all powerful.

When Moses prayed, Israel prevailed and gained great victories. When Elijah prayed God locked the heavens and it did not rain for three years. When Paul and Silas prayed the doors of the jail opened. What a power! When we pray believing today we can still see the miracles of God. Why not use the power of prayer more often?

> Nobody knows the power of prayer,
> But somebody must be listening there
> With a friendly ear for the heart that calls,
> Someone who knows when a sparrow falls.
> Miracles lie in the power of prayer;
> Faith that can banish the soul's despair!
> Hope that shines like a holy light!
> That brightens the spirit's darkest night!
> When earthly help is of no avail
> There is one Friend who will never fail;
> Just lift your eyes — the answer is there
> For nobody knows the power of prayer!

Prayer: Loving Father, life is sweet and precious when we rest in the assurance of answered prayer. Teach us more and more to implicitly trust in thy answer to our prayers being the right answer. We pray in Christ's name. Amen.

God Knows and Cares

"Are not two sparrows sold for a farthing? and one of them shall not fall on the ground without your Father."

— Matthew 10:29

How wonderful to know that God takes notice of all the small things happening on the earth! If he knows when a small sparrow falls, how much more does he take notice and care when his children are having trouble and are in need of his care.

Sitting in the waiting room of a large railway station, I watched as crowds of people swiftly passed by. "Can it be," I thought, "That God knows each one in this mass of people; knows what burdens and joys each carries in his heart, and cares about the problems?"

Yes, if God cares for the birds and the flowers he cares much more for his children.

> Why should I feel discouraged?
> Why should I feel so sad?
> For His eye is on the sparrow
> And I know He watches me.
> I sing because I'm happy,
> I sing because I'm free,
> For His eye is on the sparrow,
> And I know He watches me.

Prayer: Jesus our Saviour, give calm and sweet repose to the weary. Give thy tenderest blessings to those in want or pain. May thy angels spread their wings over those in need. We pray for Jesus' sake. Amen.

Sharing Our Heritage

"Harken to me, ye that follow after righteousness, ye that seek the Lord: look unto the rock whence ye are hewn, and to the hole of the pit whence ye are digged." — Isaiah 51:1

Knowledge of history is essential to proper appreciation and evaluation of the present. As parents it is our duty to teach our children about their forefathers. It is the duty of our children to listen.

Often our parents and grandparents had many difficulties in making a place for themselves in the world, but we have profited by a place already established for us.

Americans have a wonderful heritage. Our heritage is principles which have made our land better, our laws greater, and our economy more affluent. When we know more of our heritage we are prouder of it and more ready to uphold the traditions.

> So much the dear Saviour had done for my soul,
> I want to help other's to find Him;
> To tell how His love can a sinner make whole,
> I want to help others to find Him.
>
> 'Tis thus I can praise Him, my gratitude prove,
> I want to help other's to find Him;

In leading sad hearts to the light of his love,
I want to help others to find Him.

For this let me toil till the close of the day,
I want to help others to find Him;
For this is the work that abideth for aye,
I want to help others to find Him.

— Maud Jackson

Prayer: Our Father, we have found Jesus to be a friend ever true. May we be true to him by telling of his love. We pray in the name of Jesus. Amen.

Showing How Much We Care

"Go out into the highways and hedges, and compel them to come in, that my house may be filled." — Luke 14:23

When my husband was a very young minister he was pastor of a church in a rural community where most of the farmers kept a dairy herd. When he would ask some of them to attend services they would give the milking as an excuse. Not many had electric milkers and it was a task to milk twenty or thirty cows, bathe and dress for church, and drive several miles.

One week the young minister decided to show some of them how much he wanted them to attend the services. He went to the home of one man and helped him milk; then he went to the home of another and helped him. He was suffering the next day from sore hands but the people knew how much they were wanted and after that they managed to attend.

To me that bleeding love of his
Shall ever precious be;
Whatever He to others is,
He is the same to me.

Prayer: Our Father, renew in us again a desire to see people come to the house of the Lord. Stirred by compassion may we go out to compel the lost to come in. We pray in the name of one who said, "Whosoever will may come." Amen.

Feeding on God's Word

"And thou shalt teach them [God's words] diligently unto thy children, and shalt talk of them when thou sittest in thine house, and when thou walkest by the way, and when thou liest down, and when thou risest up." — Deuteronomy 6:7

We are to examine the truth of the things we read in the Bible. We are to teach those truths to our children.

Christianity demands belief. It demands fair examination. The man who says he is an infidel may feel differently if he reads and studies God's Word. Pride sometimes prevents people from studying and making a fair decision.

Some fail to make the proper decision toward God because they do not take the Word of God seriously.

A man walking along a sidewalk in front of a cafe was asked by another man to come in and eat. The man was very hungry but he thought the invitation was not sincere. Another begger walking along the same sidewalk was invited to come in and eat. He went in and had a sumptuous meal.

> Within this awful volume lies
>   The mystery of mysteries;
> Oh, happy they of human race,
>   To whom our God has given grace
> To hear, to fear, to read, to pray,
>   To lift the latch, to force the way;
> But better had they ne'er been born,
>   Who read to doubt, or read to scorn.

Prayer: We thank thee, our Father, for thy Holy Word, may we ever teach its precepts to our children and abide by them ourselves. We ask in the name of Christ our Lord. Amen.

Obeying God

"Hath the Lord as great delight in burnt offerings and sacrifices, as in obeying the voice of the Lord? Behold, to obey is better than sacrifice." — I Samuel 15:22

A young man went to travel in the Alps. He hired a guide. The guide told him, "If you obey me I will see that you make your trip and return safely."

The young man said that he tried in every way to obey his guide. Afterwards he said his feeling for the guide was one of deep respect and love.

Jesus said, "If ye keep my commandments, ye shall abide in my love."

Obedience is the key that unlocks the door to many things; to safety, to love, to respect, to the indwelling of Christ in our hearts.

> He does not always lead in pastures green.
> Sometimes, He who knows all

In kindness leads in weary ways
Where heavy shadows fall.

Not always by peaceful waters soft and slow,
My wandering steps he leads,
Ofttimes the heavy tempest round me blows
And darkest gloom surrounds the way.

But when the storm beats loudest
And I cannot find my way,
His hand always directs my course
To realms of brighter day.

Prayer: God, help us to be more obedient to thy will and direction. We pray in the name of Jesus Christ. Amen.

The Disease of Sin

"Everyone that is proud in heart is an abomination to the Lord: though hand join in hand, he shall not be unpunished. By mercy and truth iniquity is purged: and by the fear of the Lord men depart from evil." — Proverbs 16:5-6

I once read, "Turning green with envy has a way of making you ripe for trouble."

A woman was in the hospital dying with cancer. "If only she had submitted to surgery two years ago we could have saved her life," the doctor told her husband.

Jealousy and envy are like cancer. Unless they are cut out and thrown away at the beginning they are apt to spread and destroy us completely.

God moves in mysterious ways
His wonders to perform;
He plants his footsteps in the sea,
And rides upon the storm.

Deep in the unfathomable mines
Of never failing skill,
He treasures up his bright designs,
And works his sovereign will.
— Cowper

Prayer: Our Father, take from our hearts envy and jealousy. Help us to look only to thee for right and justice. We praise thee for the good things thou hast given us and if someone else had a little more, help us to be glad, not filled with envy. We pray in Jesus' name. Amen.

Prayer that Helps Us Forget Ourselves

"Our Father which art in heaven, Hallowed be thy name. Thy kingdom come. Thy will be done in earth, as it is in heaven.

Give us this day our daily bread. And forgive us our debts, as we forgive our debtors.

And lead us not into temptation, but deliver us from evil; For thine is the kingdom, and the power, and the glory, forever. Amen." — Matthew 6:9-13

One Sunday we were far from home and very lonely. As is our custom, we went to services in a nearby church. No one spoke to us and we felt more lonely than ever. Then came the time in the service when the congregation repeated the Lord's Prayer. We joined in and soon were so busy worshiping we forgot to be homesick.

> You cannot pray the Lord's Prayer, and even once say "I."
> You cannot pray the Lord's Prayer, and even once say "my."
> Nor can you pray the Lord's Prayer and not pray for another,
> For when you ask for daily bread, you must include your brother.
> For others are included in each and every plea;
> From the beginning to the end of it
> It does not once say "me."

Prayer: Father, make us humble, as we pray thy prayer today. Help us to think of others and their problems more each day. As Jesus was so kind and good to blot out all our sins, help us ever to be quick to forgive, and anxious to make amends. We pray in Jesus name. Amen.

Easy Just to Keep on Walking

"And Enoch walked with God: and he was not; for God took him." — Genesis 5:24

Isn't this a beautiful story. Enoch went walking with God. Wouldn't it be nice to know what they talked about! Perhaps Enoch talked of his family, maybe some problems. Maybe they talked about crops or herds of cattle. At any rate it became late and God must have said, "Come Enoch, and go home with me; it is closer to my house than yours."

We should all live so close to God that when he is ready for us to go home with him it will be easy just to keep on walking.

> The Master has gone to a distant country
>   And left me a charge to keep.
> A place in His vineyard,
>   A field of labor
> A shepherd to guard his sheep.
> May I be faithful to the work
>   He assigned me,
> Loyal in service, earnest in all
>   That I do.
>   May I be faithful,
>   Out in the field may he find me.
> When He returneth,
>   Faithful and loyal and true.

Prayer: Father, help us to remember, "Ye are not your own, ye are bought with a price, even the precious blood of Christ." Make us willing to serve in every way possible the Master who left us a charge to keep. We pray in the name of Jesus. Amen.

A Lesson from a Crust of Bread

"Behold the fowls of the air: for they sow not, nor gather into barns; yet your heavenly Father feedeth them. Are ye not much better than they?" — Matthew 6:26

This story is told of Carlyle. One day he stopped in the middle of a busy street and picked up a piece of bread that had been carelessly thrown down. He took the bread to a protected place and tenderly laid it down. "That is only a crust of bread but to a hungry dog or a bird it may mean nourishment and help."

How much more thoughtful of us is our Heavenly Father.

> All nature a sermon may preach thee;
>   The birds sing thy murmurs away —
> The birds which, nor sowing nor reaping,
>   God fails not to feed day by day;
> And He, who the creature doth cherish,
> Will He fail thee, and leave thee to perish?
>   Or are thou not better than they?
>
> God gives to each flower its rich raiment,
>   And o'er them His treasures flings free,
> Which to-day finds so fragrant in beauty,
>   And to-morrow all faded shall see.

Thus the lilies smile shame on thy care,
And the happy birds sing it to air:
Will their God be forgetful of thee?

— tr. by Mrs. Charles Spegel

Prayer: O God, we adore thee. Thou hast made the world so beautiful for us to enjoy. We thank thee that thou carest when we wander away and thou wilt call us back and forgive our mistakes. We pray in the name of Jesus. Amen.

Builders or Wreckers?

"For we are laborers together with God: ye are God's husbandry, ye are God's building." — I Corinthians 3:9

Have you ever watched two little boys playing on the floor with blocks. One child carefully stacks each block and works to make something which looks to him like a house. When he has his house just about finished the other child rushes over and kicks it down.

Life is like that. There are those who work hard to build worthwhile things. Then there are the ones who seem to get joy from being destructive. We all do well to ask ourselves the question, What type of person am I?

I watched them tearing a building down,
A gang of men in a busy town,
With a ho-heave-ho and lusty yell.
They swung a beam and the side wall fell.

I asked the foreman, "Are these men skilled,
And the men you'd hire if you had to build?
He gave a laugh and said, "No indeed!
Just common labor is all I need.
I can easily wreck in a day or two
What builders have taken a year to do."

I thought to myself as I went away,
Which of these roles have I tried to play?
Am I a builder who works with care,
Measuring life by the rule and square?
Am I shaping my deeds to a well-made plan,
    Patiently doing the best I can?
Or am I a wrecker, who walks the town,
Content with the labor of tearing down?

Prayer: Father, make us builders of thy kingdom. We ask in the name of Jesus. Amen.

Our Father's House

"Take heed therefore unto yourselves, and to all the flock, over the which the Holy Ghost hath made you overseers, to feed the church of God, which he hath purchased with his own blood."

— Acts 20:28

One Sunday I attended a church and read the following on the bulletin; "Thou art welcome, whosoever thou art that enterest this Church. It is thy Father's house: Come in the Spirit of reverence; worship in the spirit of humility; and leave it not without a prayer to God for thyself, for those who minister, and for those who worship here; then go thy way to live Christ in thy daily conduct."

I want it to be a church that is
A lamp to the path of pilgrims,
Leading them to Goodness, Truth
And Beauty. It will be good, if I am.

It is composed of people like me.
We make it what it is.
It will be friendly, if I am.
Its pews will be filled, if I
Help to fill them.

It will do a great work, if I work.

It will make generous gifts to many causes,
If I am a generous giver.

It will bring other people into
Its worship and fellowship,
If I bring others.

Therefore, with the help of God,
I shall dedicate myself to the
Task of being all of the things
That I want my church to be.

Prayer: Father, make us worthy of our church. In the name of one who gave himself for the church. Amen.

Rejoicing in God's Will

"Blessed is the man that trusteth in the Lord, and whose hope the Lord is." — Jeremiah 17:7

I rejoiced a great deal when a letter I had sent was returned to me. It was a letter to my Chaplain husband stationed in Italy. The letter had been stamped: "Returning to the states." In great rejoicing I hastened to tell all my friends and neighbors.

> If what I wish is good,
> And suits the will divine,
> By earth and hell in vain withstood
> I know it shall be mine.
> Still let them counsel take
> To frustrate His decree;
> They cannot keep a blessing back
> By heaven designed for me.
> If what my soul requires
> Evil to me would prove,
> His love shall cross my fine desires,
> His kindly-jealous Love.
>
> — Charles Wesley

Prayer: Our heavenly Father, give us the secure knowledge that where thou leadest we may safely go. Teach us to trust in thy wisdom. We pray in the name of our Saviour. Amen.

Private Worship

"As the hart panteth after the water brooks, so panteth my soul after thee, O God. My soul thirsteth for God, for the living God: when shall I come and appear before God?"

— Psalm 42:1, 2

Group worship is fine, but there are also times when we need to take time to worship alone. The means and the methods of worship are not all that is important. A person can worship at times when he is the very busiest.

Sometimes when we see some of God's beautiful handiwork in nature, on land or in the sky, we want to worship. What wonderful dividends we reap from worship. It brings a calmness of soul and spirit.

> By all means use some times to be alone;
> Salute thyself; see what thy soul doth wear;
> Dare to look in thy chest, for 'tis thine own,
> And tumble up and down what thou find'st there:
> Who cannot rest till he good fellows find,
> He breaks up house, turns out of doors his mind.
>
> — George Herbert

Prayer: Our Lord and Saviour, we pray today that we will make such desposits in thy Kingdom that we will reap dividends. Help us make preparation for a life to come. Make us friends to the friendless. Guide us in our worship to think first of others. We pray in Jesus' name. Amen.

Diamonds or Glass?

"We must all appear before the judgment seat of Christ; that every one may receive the things done in his body, according to that he hath done, whether it be good or bad."

— II Corinthians 5:10

God is still in control and in due time people will reap what they have sown.

A popular cafeteria in our city put a large number of diamond-looking stones in a jar. There were supposed to be a few real diamonds in the group. When a lady dined in the cafeteria she was allowed to pick one stone from the jar. I never heard of anyone getting a real diamond.

We sometimes think we can fool God if we look like good Christians. God looks on the heart, not appearances. He can look at the people in the world and tell the pure diamonds from the glass.

> Say where is life? It is not here I know,
> Oh! who hath power the priceless boon to give?
> All here is sorrow, sin and death and woe;
> Say where is life? for surely I would live!
> Be still, my soul, a sweet voice speaks to thee:
> "I am the Life, look up and follow Me."
>
> All that I sought, Lord, I have found in Thee,
> Thou art the way, the truth, the life.
> All that I ask for Thou hast given me.
> Well may I trust Thee, trust Thy loving heart;
> Low at Thy feet adoring do I fall,
> Own Thee my Lord, my best Beloved, my all!

Prayer: Show us the way to follow thee. We ask in the name of Jesus. Amen.

Exchange Blindness for Kindness

"Having the understanding darkened, being alienated from the life of God through the ignorance that is in them, because of the blindness of their heart." — Ephesians 5:18

The lounge was crowded. All the ladies were trying to get to the wash basins and some were almost fainting from exhaustion. A small boy was pushing about between the women, and they were becoming annoyed and impatient.

"Why should that boy be in here?" one woman asked in a rude tone of voice.

"He is blind and must stay near me," the mother spoke up in the child's defense.

First there was perfect silence. Then every woman in the room felt a burst of pity and love for the child. The women almost fell over each other to give him nickles, chewing gum, and trinkets.

We had been blind in heart!

> If you had been living when Christ was on earth,
> And had met the Saviour kind,
> What would you have asked Him to do for you,
> Supposing that you were blind?

> The child considered and then replied,
> "I suppose that without a doubt
> I'd have asked for a dog and a collar and chain
> To lead me safely about."

> And how often thus, in our faithless prayers,
> We acknowledge with shamed surprise,
> We have asked for only a collar and chain
> When we might have had our eyes!

Prayer: Our Father, give us faith to ask for the greatest things. Give us kindness of heart for those who are handicapped. We thank thee for our blessings. Our prayer is in the name of Jesus. Amen.

Expect Great Things from God

"The Lord is my strength and song, and he is become my salvation: he is my God, and I will prepare him an habitation; my father's God and I will exalt him." — Exodus 15:2

Faith in God gives us strength for the responsibilities of life.

Long ago in England there lived a man who wanted to be a missionary. Many opposed his project, but he was determined. When he made his appeal for help from the home churches he said, "Expect great things from God; attempt great things for God." We would all do well to make this our motto.

> If you are impatient, sit down and quietly talk with Job.

If you are just a little strongheaded, go and see Moses.

If you are getting weak-kneed, take a good look at Elijah.

If there is no song in your heart, listen to David.

If you are a policy man, read Daniel.

If you are getting sordid, spend a little while with Isaiah.

If you are getting chilly, get the beloved disciple, John, to put his cloak around you.

If your faith is below par, read Paul.

If you are getting lazy, watch James.

If you are losing sight of the future, climb up the stairs of Revelation and get a glimpse of the promised land.

Prayer: Our Father, give us the secret strength that comes only from thee. We ask in Jesus' name. Amen.

Peace Begins at Home

"Salt is good: but if the salt have lost his saltness, wherewith will ye season it? Have salt in yourselves, and have peace one with another." — Mark 9:50

We all love our country. We want it to be blessed and prosperous. We are willing to sacrifice for it. Yet we often complain when things are not run just as we imagine we would run them.

If we truly want peace we must love all men, regardless of color or creed.

> Is this love — the love I've taught?
> Will this carnage come to aught?
> Down the ages men have died.
> In these crusades — crucified!
> Ignoring in their greed for self —
> "Love thy neighbor as thyself."
> And the God of good above
> Pitied them, in his great love!
>
> Came the Armistice — and peace,
> From the hell of hate surcease.
> "Peace on earth good will to men" —
> Brothers, will we war again?
>   — James Edward Hungerford

Prayer: Our Father, who rules all nations, we would ask thy blessing on our nation today. May good will be restored on earth and there be peace in the nations. Often we have been selfish and obstinate. Make us gentle and kind. Bless our national leaders and lead them aright. We pray in the name of Christ our Lord. Amen.

Each Age Is Golden

"Remember now thy Creator in the days of thy youth, while the evil days come not, nor the years draw nigh, when thou shalt say, I have no pleasure in them." — Ecclesiastes 12:1

We often think of youth as the golden age of life. We should make each stage of life a golden age.

When we are children we think, "Oh, I will do great things when I am grown." When we are youths we think, "I will do wonderful things when I am away from the discipline of my parents." Then we are grown up and out of school, and we find life has more problems than we thought — but we enjoy working them out. When we are middle aged we feel it will be grand to reach retirement and have days of rest. When we are old we look back and think, "Oh, if I had my life to live over I would not make so many mistakes."

Each age is golden! We should treasure every moment.

> Does not heaven begin that day
> When the eager heart can say,
> "Surely God is in this place.
> I have seen Him face to face
> In the loveliness of flowers,
> In the service of the showers,
> And his voice has talked to me
> In the sunlit apple tree."
>
> — Bliss Carmen

Prayer: We need thee, O loving God and Father. We are often discontent and feel defeated. Make us love life as thou doth give it to us each day. Help us appreciate all good things. We ask in the name of Jesus. Amen.

Lost and Found

"I know whom I have believed, and am persuaded that he is able to keep that which I have committed unto him against that day." — II Timothy 1:12b

Tom was lost on a hunting trip. When he first realized he was lost he became frantic. Then he caught himself going in circles. When he realized this he sat down and began to repeat aloud all the verses of Scripture he could remember. He also quoted the verse above. When he had calmed himself and restored his faith he asked himself the question, "Have I tried all the ways I know to find the camp?"

"Climb a tree," seemed to come to him. Without delay he climbed the nearest tree and found he could see smoke in the distance. He was careful to mark the direction, and started walking that way. In an hour he was back with his companions.

> He leadeth me! O blessed tho't!
> O words with heavenly comfort fraught!
> What'er I do, Where'er I be,
> Still 'tis God's hand that leadeth me.
>
> And when my task on earth is done,
> When, by thy grace, the vict'ry's won,
> E'en death's cold wave I will not flee,
> Since God through Jordan leadeth me.

Prayer: Loving heavenly Father, give us the assurance of thy love and presence today. Help us to rest in the contentment of thy love and grace. We pray in the name of Jesus. Amen.

A Lot to Be Thankful For

"Enter into his gates with thanksgiving, and into his courts with praise: be thankful unto him and bless his name." — Psalm 100:4

One day when I felt especially rushed and discouraged I went to bring in the mail. There among the papers and advertisements I found a letter from a friend. It was a letter thanking us for a very small favor we had given her sometime in the past. Suddenly I didn't feel rushed at all. I wasn't so busy after all. Someone appreciated the things I was trying to do each day and had taken time to express thanks. That made the difference. What had seemed like a day of chores had suddenly become a day of opportunity.

> Not long ago when my skies were gray,
> And the smile of fortune seemed far away.
> I chided the fates that took my store
> And left me naught to be thankful for.

Came another day with a fairer sky,
As I saw my boys go tearing by —
They seemed to shout through the open door
"Say dad you have us to be thankful for."

I have the moon and the stars above
I have a home that is blessed with love
I still can smile as I did before
And that's a lot to be thankful for.

The morning sun brings another day
A time for work, a time for play
I have all these and a great deal more
Say — you have as much to be thankful for.

— Albert Roswell

Prayer: Our Father, teach us to express thankfulness for thy many blessings. We pray in Jesus' name. Amen.

Words from a Wise Man

"When I remember these things, I pour out my soul in me: for I had gone with the multitude, I went with them to the house of God, with the voice of joy and praise, with a multitude that kept holyday." — Psalm 42:4

The following passages are parts of the proclamation made by President Lincoln, October 3, 1863.

"The year that is drawing to a close has been filled with the blessings of fruitful fields and healthful skies.

"To these bounties, which are so constantly enjoyed that we are prone to forget the source from which they come, others have been added, which are of so extraordinary a nature that they cannot fail to penetrate and soften the heart which is habitually insensible to the ever watchful providence of almighty God.

"No human counsel hath devised, nor hath any mortal hand worked out these great things. They are the gracious gifts of the most high God, who, while dealing with us in anger for our sins, hath nevertheless remembered mercy.

". . . and fervently implore the interposition of the almighty hand to heal the wounds of the nation and to restore it, as soon as may be consistent with the Divine purposes, to the full enjoyment of peace, harmony, tranquility and union."

This message is still timely, is it not?

Prayer: Father, today, over a hundred years later than President Lincoln's proclamation, may we still know and honor the one God who gives us our blessings. In Christs' name. Amen.

The Gift of Technology

"And call upon me in the day of trouble: I will deliver thee, and thou shalt glorify me." — Psalm 50:15

Soon after we moved into a new home we made a trip to visit my father-in-law. He was ninety-five years old at that time. He asked all about the house and, of course, we made it sound just as nice as we thought it was. Last of all I told him about the dishwasher. He sat for a few seconds saying nothing. Then he spoke: "I wish I could have gotten one for mamma."

How well I remembered the farm kitchen with a family of six children, a mother, a father, a maiden aunt and often a hired hand. That meant piles of dishes. How wonderful it would have felt just to have a hot water heater and running water — let alone a dishwasher. I bowed my head and offered a silent prayer of thanksgiving for all our modern conveniences.

> O bless the Lord my soul!
> Nor let His mercies lie
> Forgotten in unthankfulness,
> And without praises die.

Prayer: Almighty God, our heavenly Father, help us to be ever thankful for thy multitude of blessings. For health and happiness. We pray in the name of Jesus. Amen.

Daily Blessings

"The blessing of the Lord, it maketh rich, and he addeth no sorrow with it." — Proverbs 10:22

We get so used to our everyday blessings we forget to be thankful for them. How sad God must be at times when we seem so ungrateful! Let's try to cultivate gratitude.

> Oh Lord, I thank Thee for this day
> For your great love and grace
> And for the glow of health I see
> Upon my baby's face!
>
> I thank Thee for my garden small,
> For flowers now growing there,
> It makes me mindful of my heart
> That's lost it's deep despair!

For smudges on my boy's pants
That I can wash today.
I thank Thee, Lord, most heartily.
You've washed my smudge away!

And when I sew a button on
My husband's one white shirt
I thank Thee for thy robe so white
That covers up my dirt!

Oh thank you Lord! I am not poor!
I'm rich in life and love
My home is rented here below,
But I've a mansion up above!

Prayer: Our Father, take away our preoccupation with worldly things. Make us mindful of the wise blessings thou showerest upon us each day. Give us joy in thy presence. We pray in the name of our Saviour Jesus Christ. Amen.

Life's Preciousness

"Hitherto have ye asked nothing in my name: ask, and ye shall receive, that your joy may be full." — John 16:24

Life, whether long or short, is a marvel of creation, an opportunity for service. The glorious experience called life comes our way but once. Are we grateful for it? Do we deliberately plan to make it count for the most in service and love to others.

While we are young and energetic we often fail to realize how precious life is. Then when the bloom is gone and we cannot call it back, we wish for a second chance.

There's something in the atmosphere
Around this magic time of year,
    That thrills the hearts of men,
And sort of sets the blood astir,
And makes the pulses fairly purr,
From which no doubt you will infer —
    Thanksgiving's here again!
                    — J. E. Hungerford

Prayer: Father, with thankful and humble hearts we bring our lives before thee today. We are grateful for the measure of health thou hast given us. We thank thee for all the benefits we have received from thy hand. We ask thee to take our lives and make them worth while in thy service. For we pray in the name of Jesus. Amen.

Our God Is Able

"For what thanks can we render to God again for you, for all the joy wherewith we joy for your sakes before our God."

— I Thessalonians 3:9

During a severe earthquake a few years ago the neighbors were surprised to see an elderly lady going calmy about helping the children, the young mothers, and just anyone she could find to whom she could render service.

"Grandma, aren't you afraid?" one of the children asked.

"No, if the God I worship can shake this old earth like this he certainly can take care of me."

The people hearing her took courage and their faith was strengthened.

> Help us remember
> That serving our neighbors
> Is gratitude offered
>   To Jesus, our Friend.
> For every day's blessings,
> Great without measure,
> We thank Thee and praise Thee,
>   Our Father. Amen.

Prayer: Our Father, we would thank thee that every day we have so many things for which to be thankful. We thank thee for opportunity to serve others and do good each day. Give us the wisdom to lead others in the way of thankfulness. We pray through Christ our Redeemer. Amen.

Make Every Day Thanksgiving Day

"O give thanks unto the Lord, for he is good, for his mercy endureth forever." — Psalm 107:1

When we think of Thanksgiving Day we often think of a picture so commonly seen of Pilgrims on their way to church. We see mothers and fathers and little children walking in the snow to attend worship services.

When we think of that picture and of the ways we have to travel today we should be so thankful. If our children leave home and go thousands of miles away they can still call home and talk in a matter of seconds. If there is an urgent need to get to the bedside of a loved one we can board a plane and be many hundreds of miles away in a few hours.

We give thanks to the same Lord the Pilgrims worshiped. The same Lord supplies our every need.

> Give thanks for your life as you find it;
> Thanks that there's work you can do,
> Thanks for your health, for
> The wealth of your strength, and
> The courage to battle things through.

Prayer: Oh God of Hosts, thou hast opened the windows of heaven and poured out untold blessings upon our generation. We offer thanks to thee. We thank thee for the things that make life sweet and happy. Make us worthy of thy mercies. We pray in the name of the giver of all good gifts. Amen.

Count Your Blessings

"I will remember the works of the Lord: surely I will remember thy wonders of old. I will meditate also of all thy work, and talk of thy doing." — Psalm 77:11, 12

In memory we store the joys and pleasures of the past and experiences shared with loved relatives and friends.

> These to be thankful for: a friend,
> A work to do, a way to wend,
> And these in which to take delight:
> The wind that turns the poplars white.
>
> Wonder and gleam of common things,
> Sunlight upon a sea gull's wings,
> Odors of earth and dew-drenched lawns,
> The pagentry of darks and dawns;
>
> Blue vistas of a city street
> At twilight, music, passing feet,
> The thrill of spring, half joy, half pain,
> The deep voice of the autumn rain.
>
> Shall we not be content with these
> Imperishable mysteries?
> And jocund-hearted take our share
> Of joy and pain and find life fair?

Prayer: We thank thee Father, for our beautiful world. For rich harvest and plenty of food. We thank Thee for the kind and good people who make up a majority of our population. We thank

Thee for thy love and patience with our mistakes. We pray in the name of Jesus. Amen.

Love One Another

"A new commandment I give unto you, That ye love one another; as I have loved you, that ye also love one another."
— John 13:34

Some things seem strange to us at the time they happen but God always sees what is best in accordance with his will.

Sometimes we are tempted to take the easy way out and give our love only to those who love us. We want to tell the story of Jesus only to the clean and pretty people of the world. If we follow the new commandment we will love all people.

> The camel at the close of day
> Kneels down upon the sandy plain
> To have his burden lifted off
>   And rest again.
> My soul, thou too shouldst to thy knees
> When daylight draweth to a close,
> And let thy Master lift thy load
>   And grant repose.
> Else how couldst thou the morrow meet,
> With all tomorrow's work to do,
> If thou thy burden all the night
>   Dost carry through?
> The camel kneels at break of day
> To have his guide replace his load,
> Then rises up anew to take
>   The desert road.
> So thou shouldst kneel at morning's dawn
> That God may give thee daily care
> Assured that He no load too great
>   Will make thee bear.

Prayer: Father, we would pour ourselves out in thy service. Use us today. For we ask in Jesus' name. Amen.

Seedtime and Harvest

"In the morning sow thy seed, and in the evening withhold not thine hand." — Ecclesiastes 11:6

How fine it is when we are young to sow good seed — seeds of helpfulness and kindness; seeds of sharing and improving the world about us.

A man I knew worked very hard as a young man trying to invent machinery that would make the farmer's work easier. In a measure he succeeded. When he was old his health was very poor, but he had plenty to live on because the royalties from his inventions kept coming in.

We dropped the seed o'er hill and plain,
    Beneath the sun of May,
And frightened from our sprouting grain
    The robber crows away.

And now, with autumn's moonlit eves,
    Its harvest time has come,
We pluck away the frosted leaves,
    And bear the treasure home.

Then shame on all the proud and vain,
    Whose folly laughs to scorn
The blessing of the hardy grain,
    Our wealth of golden corn!

Heap high the farmer's wintry hoard!
    Heap high the golden corn!
No richer gift has Autumn poured
    From out her lavish horn!

But let the good old crop adorn
    The hills our fathers trod;
Still let us, for his golden corn,
    Send up our thanks to God!

Prayer: Our Father, we thank thee for our new age, for new visions of feats to accomplish. We thank thee for fresh opportunities to gather harvest from seed sown by our fathers. Amen.

Using Each Day Well

"The Lord hath done great things for us; whereof we are glad." — Psalm 126:3

"I will remember the years of the right hand of the Most High." — Psalm 77:10

We do not understand some of the errors we have made. This is a busy age. Perhaps we made some mistakes because we did not take time to think and meditate. We cannot undo the past, but we can ask God to help us make the future better. All of life is hastening to fulfill its mission. Let us go our way with enthusiasm.

Only a day of life, soon to be done,
'Tis passing now to die at set of sun.
Only a day, but fraught with vital things;
Issues of Life and Death each hour brings.

Only a Day! But as each moment flies
Some earth-worn pilgrim folds his arms and dies.
Only a Day! Only a breath of time,
Yet filled with opportunities sublime.

If this one day shall thus be spent for him,
New joy shall come to saint and seraphim;
In earth and heaven the choirs of God will sing,
As to the cross the lost ones we shall bring.

Then count each day a part of God's great plan;
Use well its hours to help your fellow man;
Time is the stuff of which our lives are made,
And when 'tis lost all mankind are betrayed.

Prayer: Our Father, we come with deepest gratitude to thank thee for the many great things thou hast done for us. In the name of Christ we pray. Amen.

Keep On Walking

"We walk by faith, not by sight." — II Corinthians 5:7

A ten-year-old boy was lost in the woods. One minute he had been with his father and brother; the next he had wandered away and could not find them again. He called and called but the rustle of the leaves drowned out his calls. All night long he wandered around. He was very cold but he kept walking, shaking his arms and legs. Early the next morning he put his ear to the ground as he had heard about Indians doing. He thought he heard the sound of a big truck. Sure enough as he walked and listened he soon found a road. A short time later a car picked him up and he was soon re-united with his loved ones.

Often we come to a place when we want to give up. If we just keep walking, working, and listening for the voice of God we will come to a place of safety.

> God has given you His promise,
>   That He hears and answers prayer:
> He will heed your supplication,
>   If you cast on Him your care.

Prayer: Thou who didst redeem us, hear our call today. Make us true followers of thine. Give us courage to keep walking when the way is rough. We pray in the name of Jesus. Amen.

Remembering to Give Thanks

"In everything give thanks: for this is the will of God in Christ Jesus concerning you." — I Thessalonians 5:18

A little child went to visit some friends. At the table the family she was visiting started noisily passing the food. Noticing the little visitor was not eating, the mother in the home asked, "Aren't you hungry, dear?"

"Oh, yes, I am hungry, but I always wait for the food to be blessed."

The children of the home looked at her, ashamed; the parents were aghast. "Will you bless the food for all of us?"

The little child said the little verse her mother had taught her;

Father we thank Thee for the night,
And for the pleasant morning light;
For rest and food and loving care,
And all that makes the world so fair.

Help us to do the things we should,
To be to others kind and good;
In all we do, in work or play,
To love Thee better day by day.

— Rebecca J. Weston

Prayer: How shall we thank thee, Lord, for all thy abundant mercies; for friendships, homes, true kindness of friends. Be near to guide us today, we pray in the name of Christ our Lord. Amen.

Happy to Help

"Blessed is he that considereth the poor: the Lord will deliver him in time of trouble." — Psalm 41:1

There were two stores in a small town. One store had an easy-going owner who was always trying to serve his customers better. If he could help someone by going a few blocks out of the way he didn't mind. The other storekeeper was just the opposite. Every aim and plan was to make more profit. One year, times were very hard and more and more people had come to the easy-going storekeeper and asked for credit. People said, "He will surely have to go out of business if he doesn't stop helping people." But the kindly man managed to keep his doors open and he was happy to be able to help others.

> Great God of Nations, now to Thee,
>   Our hymn of gratitude we raise;
> With humble heart and bending knee
>   We offer Thee our song of praise.
>
> Thy name we bless, Almighty God,
>   For all the kindness Thou has shown
> To this fair land the Pilgrims trod —
>   This land we fondly call our own.
>
> We praise Thee that the Gospel's light
>   Through all our land it's radiance sheds
> Dispels the shade of error's night,
>   And heavenly blessings around us spreads.
>
> Great God, preserve us in Thy fear;
>   In danger, still our Guardian be;
> O spread Thy truth's bright precepts here;
>   Let all the people worship Thee.

Prayer: Our God, help us to have assurance of thy love and care. We ask in Jesus' name. Amen.

In Everything Give Thanks

"It is a good thing to give thanks unto the Lord." — Psalm 92:1
"Let us come before his presence with thanksgiving, and make a joyful noise unto him with psalms." — Psalm 95:2

The Bible admonishes us to be thankful. As Americans we set aside a certain day in which to proclaim our thanks to God for his goodness.

We should always give thanks to God. He does not confine his blessings to just one day each year but pours them out each day we live.

Dr. Torrey, a minister, told the story of a young university student who saved seventeen men from drowning. When he became exhausted and could swim no longer the boy kept saying, "Did I do my best?"

Later, in a revival service, Dr. Torrey was told that the boy was in the services. He asked him to come forward and testify. Asked if any one thing stood out in the experience, the young man replied, "Not one of the seventeen thanked me."

111

Grave on thy heart each past "red-letter day"!
Forget not all the sunshine of the way
By which the Lord hath led thee: answered prayers,
And joys unasked, strange blessings, lifted cares,
Grand promise-echoes! Thus thy life shall be
One record of His love and faithfulness to thee.

— F. R. Havergal

Prayer: Lord, we thank thee for the Thanksgiving heritage. Make us worthy of the example of our forefathers. We pray in the name of Jesus. Amen.

Our Precious Companion

"If a man love me, he will keep my words: and my Father will love him, and we will come unto him, and make our abode with him." — John 14:23

My son had just returned from two years of military service, much of which had been spent in Germany. He found things at home changed and strange. He decided to go to a religious retreat in the mountains. The second day he returned home.

"It is lonely in a crowd when you do not know any of the people," he explained.

If we love God he will abide with us and we will always have a precious companion.

> Pray, don't find fault with the man who limps,
>   Or stumbles along the road,
> Unless you have worn the shoes he wears
>   Or struggled beneath his load.
> There may be tacks in his shoes that hurt
>   Though hidden away from view,
> Or the burdens he bears placed on your back
>   Might cause you to stumble, too.
> Don't sneer at the man who's down today,
>   Unless you have felt the blow
> That caused his fall, or felt the shame
>   That only the fallen know.
> You may be strong but still the blows
>   That were his, if dealt to you
> In the selfsame way at the selfsame time,
>   Might cause you to stagger, too.
> Don't be too harsh with the man who sins,
>   Or pelt him with words or stones,

Unless you are sure, yea, doubly sure,
That you have not sins of your own.

Prayer: Help us to see that all things work together for good to them that love thee. In Christ's name. Amen.

God's Windows

"Gracious is the Lord, and righteous; yea, our God is merciful."
— Psalm 116:5

A little girl walking around the block with her father noticed the moon and stars shining very brightly.

"Look, daddy, God has washed his windows. See how bright his lights are."

We should feel as near to God and that God is as real at all times, as the little one felt on that clear night.

Let him who would deny that God is real
Out into the night with heart uplifted steal.
And see the wonders of the heavens above,
To be convinced of God's eternal love.

The moon and stars proclaim His wondrous power
And all of nature sings of Him each hour.
Dear God, teach us that Thou hast made Thy plan
An everlasting benediction to man.

Teach us to glorify Thy name
Through worship of This only Son
The wonders of Thy love proclaim
Each day as victory is won.

Prayer: Dearest Lord, help us to feel the comfort of thy presence. May we always know that thou art real and very near. Give us joy in this knowledge. We ask in the name of Jesus. Amen.

Rest for Our Souls

"When he giveth quietness, who then can make trouble? and when he hideth his face who then can behold him? whether it be done against a nation, or against a man only." — Job 34:29

The year had been long and we were physically exhausted. For our vacation we drove up into the mountains and enjoyed the quiet of nature. On Sunday we attended a small country church where we heard a good sermon. God gave rest and quietness to our souls as well as to our bodies.

I needed the quiet, so He drew me aside
Into the shadows where we could confide;
Away from the bustle where all the day long
I hurried and worried when active and strong.

I needed the quiet, though at first I rebelled,
But gently, so gently, my cross He upheld;
And whispered so sweetly of spiritual things;
Though weakened in body, my spirit took wings
To heights never dreamed of when active and gay,
He loved me so gently, He drew me away.

I needed the quiet, No prison my bed,
But a beautiful valley of blessing instead:
A place to grow richer, in Jesus to hide,
I needed the quiet, so He drew me aside.

— A. H. Mortenson

Prayer: Our Father, when we turn aside and spend a quiet time with thee, our hope and courage are renewed. We ask thee to grant us grace to face life's problems. Fill us with a desire to be alone with thee some part of each day. Through Jesus Christ we pray. Amen.

Remembrances

"And when he had given thanks, he brake it, and said, Take, eat: this is my body, which is broken for you: this do in remembrance of me. After the same manner also he took the cup, when he had supped, saying, This cup is the new testament in my blood: this do ye, as oft as ye drink it in remembrance of me."

— I Corinthians 11:24, 25

Baptism and the Lord's Supper belong together. They have to do with the same event, the resurrection of Christ.

Several years ago my husband and I bought some cemetery lots and paid them out by the month. We did not want our children burdened with making that choice after we were gone. We always planned we would also buy a headstone but never have had time for that. People just want some way to be remembered when they are gone from this earth.

Jesus planned a Supper for us to remember him by. How precious the observance of that supper is to his redeemed children.

Could we with ink the ocean fill,
And were the sky of parchment made

Were every blade of grass a quill,
    And every man a scribe by trade;
To write the love of God with ink
Would drain the ocean dry;
    Nor would the scroll
    Contain the whole,
Though spread from sky to sky.

Prayer: Father, may we often examine our hearts and see if we are keeping the right memory of our Lord and Saviour. Keep us by thy love and guidance close to thee. We pray in the name of Jesus. Amen.

The Good Life

"But God commendeth his love toward us, in that, while we were yet sinners, Christ died for us." — Romans 5:8

Two friends of mine just back from a trip to twelve foreign countries told me the following story.

Just a few days before they were to leave for home Lou became ill. She knew she must have help or she could not start home. They found their way to a doctor's office in West Berlin. The doctor was very efficient and quickly located a kidney infection. As the doctor worked he said several times, "Ah, in America you have the good life."

As they winged their way home a few days later they looked down from the plane on the beautiful clouds and thanked God for letting them live in America. They had not realized before how good God had been to them.

For the love of God is broader
    Than the measure of man's mind,
And the heart of the Eternal
    Is most wonderfully kind.

If our love were but more simple,
    We should take him at his word,
And our lives would be all sunshine
    In the sweetness of our Lord.
                                    — F. W. Faber

Prayer: Loving heavenly Father, teach us to love as thou hast loved. Make us willing to think of others first. Fill us with a desire to serve mankind. We pray in the name of Jesus. Amen.

Words of Encouragement

"Behold thou hast instructed many, and thou hast strengthened the weak hands. Thy words have upholden him that was falling, and thou hast strengthened the feeble knees." — Job 4:3, 4

When I was twenty-five years old we lived in an apartment attached to a store. We took turns running the little store and going to school, the Southwestern Baptist Seminary at Fort Worth, Texas. To many, I am sure, it looked as if we were having a hard time. We had three small children, only one old enough for kindergarden. My husband's youngest sister also lived with us and she also went to school part time.

One day a young minister came into the store. A church he had felt sure would call him, had called another man. He was so blue he had decided to give up and quit school. I talked very earnestly to him about how God upholds those who follow him. He soon left but I think the picture of three young people and three children making out as best they could with the pennies and dimes from milk and bread sales helped him. He went back to school and later was called to serve a church. Sometimes a word of encouragement is worth a great deal.

> Yet I argue not
> Against Thy hand or will, nor bate a jot
> Of heart or hope, but still bear up and steer
> Right onward.
>
> — John Milton

Prayer: Father, fill us with words of courage, In Jesus' name we pray. Amen.

Cheering Us On

"Thou shalt worship the Lord thy God, and him only shalt thou serve." — Matthew 4:10

None of us like to taste the humiliation of defeat. We like to have our children win when they are in contest. We like to have our team win in games. Our heavenly Father likes to have us win a victory over temptation. He is there on the side line watching and pushing for us to be victorious. Perhaps if we remember he is for us it will help us turn aside temptation and win a victory.

> Never a trial that He is not there;
> Never a burden that He doth not bear;
> Never a sorrow that He doth not share.
> Moment by moment I'm under his care.

116

Never a heart-ache, and never a groan,
Never a tear-drop, and never a moan,
Never a danger but there, on the throne,
Moment by moment, He thinks of his own.

Never a weakness that He doth not feel;
Never a sickness that He cannot heal.
Moment by moment, in woe or in weal,
Jesus, my Saviour, abides with me still.

— Daniel W. Whittle

Prayer: Almighty God, our heavenly Father, we confess that we are often tempted to sin. We often forget to pray before we make decisions. Help us to turn to thee and find strength to resist temptation, peace in our hearts and the light of hope. We ask in the name of Christ. Amen.

God Is "Holding the Rope"

"He shall not be afraid of evil tidings: his heart is fixed, trusting in the Lord." — Psalm 112:7

In the mountains of a foreign land some men and boys were standing near a precipice. A climber had become lost and was stranded down below. The men were talking of a way to get a rope to the man below and lift him out.

"You are light and small, Jack. Will you let us tie a rope around you and send you down?"

The shepherd lad drew back in fear, "Oh no!" he cried. Then he saw his father coming across the field. "I will gladly go if my daddy holds the rope."

We need not be afraid in this world of evil and trouble so long as our Father holds the rope.

This is my Father's world,
    And to my listening ears,
All nature sings, and round me rings
    The music of the spheres.

This is my Father's world,
    I rest me in the thought
Of rocks and trees, of skies and seas
    His hand the wonders wrought.

This is my Father's world,
    O let me ne'er forget

That though the wrong seems oft so strong,
    God is the ruler yet.
                  — Maltie D. Babcock

Prayer: Most Gracious Father, we feel that thou art never far from us. We count it a dear privilege to be able to call thee Father. May we ever trust in thy care. Amen.

Unselfish Prayer

"If ye then, being evil, know how to give good gifts unto your children, how much more shall your Father which is in heaven give good things to them that ask him?" — Matthew 7:11

> These are the gifts I ask
> Of thee, Spirit serene:
> Strength for the daily task,
> Courage to face the road,
> Good cheer to help me bear the traveler's load,
> And for the hours of rest that come between,
> An inward joy in all things heard and seen.
> These are the sins I fain
> Would have thee take away:
> Malice, and cold disdain,
> Hot anger, sullen hate,
> Scorn of the lowly, envy of the great,
> And discontent that casts a shadow gray
> On all the brightness of a common day.
>   — Henry Van Dyke

Sometimes we pray for our loved ones and we ask God to give them certain gifts. Oftentimes they are selfish requests. We should always remember to ask that God's will be done in the matter of gifts.

Linda was used to her father leaving on Monday mornings for business trips. One Monday when he was going to a foreign land he asked her what she would like to have him bring her. She thought of all the things she had heard about foreign countries and her little heart trembled with fear.

"Just bring back my daddy to me," she told him.

Her father was so pleased at this request made from a heart of love that he took special pains on his trip to select Linda a beautiful doll dressed in native costume.

Prayer: Dear Lord, if our prayers are selfish, forgive us. May our requests be made subject to thy will. Amen.

Searching for Samaria

"The woman then left her waterpot, and went her way into the city, and saith to the men, Come, see a man, which told me all things that ever I did: is not this the Christ? Then they went out of the city, and came unto him." — John 4:28, 29, 30

When Jesus met the woman at the well and she trusted and believed him to be the Christ, he did not send her to some distant city to witness. She went into her own city where people knew all about her sinful life. There she told the men about Jesus and brought them to him.

There is a Samaria for each child of God; a place where he especially wants us to witness for him. Are we finding our Samaria, or are we waiting for a chance to go to some far away place and tell the story?

We have a friend who wanted very much to become a minister when he was a young High School student. For some reason he never studied theology, nor did he make an effort to become a minister. Often he told friends how he felt called. When a new minister came to the church he told him about his desire to become a minister. The new minister immediately led the church to start a mission to a minority group. He appointed this man to fill the pulpit on Sundays until the mission grew strong enough to hire a pastor. That frustrated man soon was happy serving in his own Samaria. He had not really looked for it before.

We must each search for a place to serve. Christ will lead us to the right Samaria.

Prayer: Father, may we be zealous in our search for a place of service, if it be thy will. Amen.

Fishers of Men

"And he saith unto them, Follow me, and I will make you fishers of men. And they straightway left their nets, and followed him." — Matthew 4:19, 20

We can picture James and John as they go to their father Zebedee, "Father we are going to follow Jesus and be fishers of men."

I am sure Zebedee hated to see his boys go. They had worked so closely together on the boat, to make a living. Yet I cannot think they left without first winning their father to Christ. Perhaps he was proud that the Master had called his fine young sons to be followers.

As God leads I am content;
   He will take care!
All things by his will are sent
   That I must bear;
To him I take my fear,
My wishes, while I'm here;
The way will all seem clear,
   When I am there!
As God leads me so my heart
   In faith shall rest.
No grief nor fear my soul shall part
   From Jesus' breast.
In sweet belief I know
What way my life doth go —
Since God permitteth so —
   That must be best.

— L. Gedicke

Prayer: O Lord, direct us in all our following. Give us favor and grace as we seek to be fishers of men. May we glorify thy Holy name. We ask in the name of Jesus. Amen.

Losing Sight of the Goal

"Simon Peter saith unto them, I go a fishing. They say unto him, We also go with thee. They went forth, and entered into a ship immediately; and that night they caught nothing."

— John 21:3

Peter and the disciples seemed to have lost sight of the fact that they had twice seen the risen Lord. They had forgotten there was a kingdom to be expanded for the Lord, and that they were the ones he had selected to build that kingdom on earth. They gave up and decided to go fishing.

How often we lose sight of our goal in serving Christ and just go fishing after worldly pleasures and activities. Next morning the sight of the Lord on the sea shore brought them back to their task.

Whether you'll try for the goal that's afar
Or be contented to stay where you are.
Take it or leave it. Here's something to do,
Just think it over. It's all up to you!
What do you wish? To be known as a shirk;
Known as a good man who's willing to work,
Scorned for a loafer or praised by your chief,
Rich man or poor man or begger or thief?

Eager or earnest or dull through the day,
Honest or crooked? It's you who must say!
You must decide in the face of the test
Whether you'll shirk it or give it your best.

Prayer: Our Gracious heavenly Father, keep us from going astray after things of the world. Give us strength of character to decide on the path of service for thee. We pray in the name of our Great Redeemer. Amen.

Was It You?

"For ye were sometimes darkness, but now are ye light in the Lord: walk as children of light." — Ephesians 5:8

Sin leaves a mark on all of us. A woman was brutally murdered on the campus of a great school. A feeling of fear went over the whole town because no one knew who the murderer might be. Some perverted mind in the school took delight in writing ugly things on waste baskets and walls. When at last the criminal was caught tensions relaxed and people acted more normal.

Someone started the whole day wrong —
    Was it you?
Someone robbed the day of it's song —
    Was it you?
Early this morning someone frowned;
Someone sulked until others scowled;
And soon harsh words were passed around —
    Was it you?

Someone started the day aright —
    Was it you?
Someone made it happy and bright —
    Was it you?
Early this morning, we are told,
Someone smiled and all through the day —
This smile encouraged young and old —
    Was it you?

Prayer: Our Father, direct our paths today. Give us a gracious attitude toward all we meet. Make our words pleasing to thee. May we glorify thy name by our deeds. We pray through Jesus Christ, our Lord. Amen.

Ready for the End

"For he saith, I have heard thee in a time accepted, and in the day of salvation have I succored thee: behold, now is the day of salvation." — II Corinthians 6:2

Time is always speeding on. No one can promise you another day of life. We must trust God for that. We should finish any tasks we feel important today. Most of all we must see that we are right with God. It is always later than we think. We should be ready at all times for the end of life for us.

> Dream not too much of what you'll do tomorrow,
> How well you'll work perhaps another year;
> Tomorrow's chance you do not need to borrow —
> Today is here.
>
> Boast not too much of mountains you will master,
> The while you linger in the vale below;
> To dream is well, but plodding brings us faster
> To where we go.
>
> Talk not too much about some new endeavor
> You mean to make a little later on;
> Who idles now will idle on forever
> Till life is done.
>
> Swear not some day to break some habit's fetter,
> When this old year is dead and passed away;
> If you have need of living wiser, better,
> Begin today!

Prayer: Father, make us conscious of the time of our lives fleeting away. May we prepare for all tomorrows. We ask in Christ's name. Amen.

Wasted Moments

"He left nothing undone of all that the Lord commanded Moses." — Joshua 11:15

As each day passes we do not notice the wasted minutes, but if all were added up and presented to us at one time we would be shocked to see how much time we had spent in careless idleness — time we could have spent accomplishing the tasks we omitted.

> Although some seeds are wasted and some work destroyed by gale,

Some crops yield unexpectedly, while others seem to
    fail.
Yet there must be a harvest, the fulfillment of our toil,
The goodness will be gathered after patience from the
    soil.

And life, too, has a harvest for the aims that we pursue,
Although some good deeds planted do not flourish it is
    true.
Some plans are disappointing, sown too early or too
    late,
While impulses of kindness might grow friendships that
    are great.

In nature and in life we plan our way and sow our seeds,
But in God's time and season reap the harvest of our
    deeds.

— Kathleen Partridge

Prayer: May the harvest we reap each year be fruitful. Forgive us the omissions we have made. In Jesus' name. Amen.